For long periods of time my life has been LONELIER THAN DEATH.

The eighth, and final collection of poetry and writing from the long-suffering PHIL FLETCHER.

('The Chinese read the time in the eyes of cats'. Baudelaire.)

I'm going to dedicate this collection to Enoch Soames, a character created by Max Beerbohm, for reasons that would be clear to anyone who's read this entertaining tale entitled: 'Enoch Soames': 'Let creation be its own reward'.

...

'When suffering and blight continue beyond all logical reasoning, you can only conclude that unnatural, dark forces are at work, to keep you pinned down in a labyrinthine nightmare'. Phil Fletcher.

I wonder if this theory of mine could knock Steven Hawking's 'A BRIEF HISTORY OF TIME' into a cocked hat: 'But in Space, time is of no consequence'; there, it's as simple as that. Phil Fletcher.

..

Every day I pray to the Great Spirit for the energy and serenity needed to cope with the hellish agony that is my loveless (I'd settle for sex and affection) and socially isolated existence; are all the real Bohemians really dead? (Cried out in an anguished manner for added effect.)

THIS IS A BLACK SUN PRESS PRODUCTION BY PHIL FLETCHER, FOR PHIL FLETCHER

(There's a big market out there for people's misery, misfortune, and madness; [what other excuse could there be for the likes of RADIOHEAD, COLDPLAY, AND MORRISEY?] And I want a piece of this hardcore, hot, money changing hands, action.)

Fit young women are from Venus, older, and old women are like creatures from the BLACK LAGOON; a totally alien species. Phil (Vincent Heathcliff) Fletcher.

...

PHILIP FLETCHER

THE BLACK SUN Epress

LTD (LONELIER THAN DEATH.)

ISBN 978-09556879-2-1

Published by Lulu.com

Partial credit to K for useful help in finalising this project.

LIVERPOOL'S 'YEAR OF CULTURE', 2008.

Both Liverpool and football are boring beyond compare,
A broad Scouse accent makes me go limp with despair;
I'm certain it's only other murderers of the English language who will go there during their derisory year of 'culchair'. (Update, I've heard it's preparations are coming apart at the seams. 13/7/06.)

……………………………………………………………………….

'Hey! If you can't get to the Hay on Wye literary fest, try hay on rye, it's dry man, it's dry.

………………………………………………………………………….

'Your life is an unmitigated pile of shite, therefore you should do the decent thing and top yourself…discuss'.
'Er…what about really old people that refuse to die (like my dad, he's 88 now, the old coffin dodger), and whom the government keeps throwing wasted money at? They should be made to take the 'exit pill' or else live on survival rations'.

…………………………………………………………………………...

THERE'S A YAWNING GULF BETWEEN FELIX DENNIS AND MYSELF. (He sends me to sleep every time I hear his poetry.)

Getting freebies out of Dennis Publishing is my delight,
Because as a poet, Felix is SHITE! I bet you daren't publish this letter in VIZ, it wud be too dizrespekful to the 6-10th's billionaire-head; I wish he'd sue me instead so I cud get sum free pub grub and publicity…you see I'm an undi'scuppered' modern poet…Me!

The 25th Collectors edition of Viz is great, it's all 'toons and no boring word pages mate, and you can use that bird on the front cover as a wank fantasy 2 or 3 times a day; I do anyway.

Cunnilingua Franka. ('Me name's Frank…geddit'?)

………………………………………………………………………….

For Gaia Holmes, poetess, and one-time bane of my existence, who accused me of ranting in my work the last time I had the misfortune to clap eyes on her. 'Rant' rhymes with (you) 'cant', (there is such a word, check it out), the same as 'hunt' rhymes with..

..

..

..RUNT!

One definition of the word 'cant' is 'argot of the underworld', I like the word 'argot'.

..

What follows is a copy of an e-mail I sent to the Sylvia Plath Forum some time ago:

'Hi, I was introduced to Sylvia Plath's work some 15 years ago by someone who is, by nature, more miserable than me. I began to 'hoover up' Sylvia's poetry, hating the earlier 'flowery' stuff, but really appreciating her later 'cosmically aware' work, when she was close to self-destruction; I read her collected letters too.

I was so depressed myself once that I fantasised about going up to her grave site on a really cold, moonlit winter's night, with a bottle of Southern Comfort, getting blotto, and freezing to death beneath her headstone; what a way to go, ay!? But, like the proverbial Weir wolf, I'm all right nowwwwOOOOOOO!!! Too much lack of success in my chosen field of modern 'existential' poetry, makes me feel periodically suicidal, like 'Suicidal Sid' out of Viz comic. I'm sure if Sylvia was still alive she'd take me to her bosom and champion my cause as a believer in the right to say whatever the hell I please; and go into hiding 'on't tops', and freeze and starve to death up there if anyone took violent exception to my views. And there are plenty of you out there, aren't there? Ready to take up the cudgels at the slightest provocation.

As a severely disabled person, I write to relieve my distress at living in such a god-awful stage in human dissolution; 'Yeah, I was a young man back in the 1960s', and it was a lot freer (not Greer) then than it is now. 'Who are the thought police', and why are they here in England's 'green with envy', 'look down on peasants', land? I wonder how many of you will read this 'voice in the wilderness' of cyber-space, need to communicate, plea for acknowledgement of my existence, missive?

Maybe even Sylvia will read it on her lap-top up there in the pantheon of the literary Gods...and not be too dismissive?

'DON'T PANIC JOHHNY IN THE BABEL OF BAD DREAMS AND BLIGHT SCARES'. Phil Fletcher/aka: Vincent Heathcliff.

'I'M GETTING AWAY WITH IT!'
(To 'contemporary artists' everywhere.)

'Yeah, I'm getting away with it, churning out crap, and what's more to the point, I'M GETTING PAID FOR IT!!!!!'
True art is dead, but it doesn't stop these bozo's making 'bread' out of its bloated and rotten corpse, and claiming legitimacy while they're screwing it.
Man reached the highest point in his artistic endeavours, musically and painting-wise, in the 18th and 19th centuries; you can't go any exultantly higher than Beethoven's 9th Symphony, as well as his other eight, as well as all the other great composers. Now all we have are posers who seem to hate life, and are doing their worst to murder the image of heavenly music with their dark, putrid dirges, and tuneless, toneless diatribes.
Modern art is a manifestation of the Id, with delusions of grandeur; but if nobody bought this diseased rubbish, it would be forced to retreat back to the primordial swamp where the Id belongs; is 'Id' short for Idiot?
But hey! It's not all doom and dismay, 20th century English literature (as well as 19th century French) has been the best ever; my own efforts, sadly unsung, included; even this piece which I've extruded from a disillusioned intellect, after seeing an elected spokesperson for contemporary art sounding off on 'Richard & Judy'; two prime examples of our, 'I'm getting away with it, and what's more, I'm getting obscenely well paid for it' culture.
I've spent a good part of my life reading, it's been a largely stimulating and exhilarating substitute for a happy, healthy, 'normal' existence; I was an avid reader long before I knew I wanted to be a writer. I love the English language when it's telling a good story, like: 'THE ANGEL AND THE CUCKOO' by Gerald Kersh, or 'THE DEVILS OF LOUDON' by Aldous Huxley.
And this England, my 'birth' country, has done its best to kill me, its native born son; only now the things I loved about it have gone; I'm ready to move on, maybe as early as next year, there's nothing left (except poverty) to keep me here.
In the last 24 hours, there've been 2 fatal stabbings, and 2 near fatal stabbings here in affluent England; one near fatal stabbing just minutes from where I live, and one fatal stabbing in a wealthy suburb in Chelse;, (maybe they'll employ private security in Chelsea from now on?) And the other murder was a 15-year-old schoolboy in Manchester; a whole host of lives in ruin and turmoil because of acts of impetuous stupidity (gratuitous nihilism). At least if I die now, prematurely, before I'm at least 85, I will have 'enjoyed' the youthful magical and mystical period of my life (mostly on my own, never having known 'young [and requited] love'); there's only two-way love left for me to enjoy now, and hopefully, not with a lady-boy. Phil Fletcher. 30/11/04.

………………………………………………………………………………

STUCK INSIDE A HOTEL ROOM IN LIMMASOL, WITH THE 'WHAT THE FUCK AM I DOING HERE' BLUES AGAIN.

A lot of us keep ourselves alive because we don't fancy the other, ultimate alternative; it's not so much the quality of our lives that counts, but merely keeping ourselves out of the ground or the incinerator.
Late last September, or early October, I began to have pangs of pre-Christmas gloom, should I spend it here on my own, or should I look for a brighter option? I opted for the latter choice, my decision strongly influenced by the very inconsiderate behaviour of a woman who runs a dance school above my flat, causing horrendous noise nuisance because she's been too mean to install any insulation between our two properties. Her reign of terror is gradually being brought under control by our local environmental health dept, who are getting tired of her 'extracting the urine'.
I spotted an ad' in a daily paper for what looked like a good holiday package in Limassol, Cyprus. I've never been to Cyprus, so I checked this package out on the Internet, and booked 2 weeks escape from pressure of all kinds, on my credit card.
By the morning of 15th December, departure day, I felt thoroughly burnt-out from accumulated stress, caused by the herd of stampeding buffaloes above me; four nights a week and all day Saturday. And even though I'm now a veteran air traveller, I still always think that my next flight will be my last, due to the plane crashing. Apart from this morbid fear, I can't recommend flying highly enough, (no pun intended.)
It's over 2000 miles to Cyprus, we covered that in four hours; by the time I'd unpacked everything and put it away in my depressing hotel room, and figured out how to work the ancient 14-inch screen TV, it was 1 am, Cyprus time. I was due to meet Despo, our holiday rep, at 9.15am in the morning.
I booked up for 3 trips through the smoulderingly attractive Despo, who called me 'my dear', (I instantly thought she fancied me) and that was the last I saw of her during my entire holiday.
I discovered in Limassol that the term 'sandy beach' can cover a multitude of sins; in this case it was a narrow strip of black sand strewn with rocks and pebbles. Limassol has got everything a tourist needs, if you're prepared to go out and take advantage of it; blaming my severe visual handicap, (I don't feel safe walking on the pavement after dark), I wasn't. There was a pub called THE SHIP INN less than 10 minutes walk away, boasting live music, etc, but I couldn't get myself motivated enough to go and check it out. Doh!
I enjoyed my day trips, apart, mainly, from when we had to get off the coach and wander about till it was time to get back on it again; once for 3 hours! ('3 hours! What am I going to find to do for the next 3 hours!!?') The Troodos mountains are well worth a visit, but everywhere else I went was spoilt because of insane levels of traffic.

At nearly 58, I was one of the youngest guests in our hotel, which, fortunately for me, wasn't very full. The dining room was a very dimly lit cavern, I could hardly see what choice of fare was on offer when there wasn't a set main course; and at 7pm each evening there was a thinly disguised stampede by the ancient guests to get in there and get stuck in. I did a lot of 'comfort' over-eating, and suffered accordingly. By Dec. 24th I would gladly have come home if it would had been financially possible, but I had another 5 days to endure. I declined the Xmas Eve Gala dinner, preferring to eat chocolate and sip some very palatable Cyprus brandy in my bleak room, trying to make some sense out of Greek TV. I couldn't, and I was glad for any English-speaking films I could find. Christmas day is a blank, I remember having breakfast and that's about it, I know I felt very depressed and wished I was dead...
I've now sworn never to do anything on impulse ever again; the whole sorry saga has cost me around £600. 12/1/05.

..

AMYGDALA RHYMES WITH CALIGULA, (and he was a total nutter wasn't he?) (WHAT YOU DON'T KNOW.)

They say that what you don't know can't hurt you, but when it comes to easy-to-procure health supplements that you just didn't know the benefits of, due to ignorance or lack of access to the relevant information, until after you've needlessly suffered needless discomfort for most of your 58-years of life...then it hurts BIG TIME!
I'm talking about basic things like glucosamine and aloe vera capsules (as long as they don't contain a peppermint additive), pollen extract and saw palmetto, and the marvellous St. John's Wort, oh, and calcium. Of course, none of these beneficent health aids can really compensate for a fairly unrelenting, harsh, and unforgiving existence; and the really harmful effects this condition will have on your physical and mental health.
When I say 'harsh and unrelenting', I'm talking in terms of the context of being born a 'free' man in a 'free' society. Does my suffering social isolation, persecution and rejection over the last 35 years of my 'life', equate with the suffering of someone who survived 18 months in the nazi's most notorious death camp, Auschwitz, and who, 60 years on can still remember vividly what went on there? You would probably say I don't have a leg to stand on, but unless you've experienced some 35 years of waking up on your own on Christmas Day morning, with nothing but a hangover for company for most of them, and no presents; and unless you've been rejected by every woman (in my case) you ever fell in love with, and made to feel your not worthy or fit to

be a father because of disabilities; and that your writing is sub-standard because you can't get a major publishing house (how come Philip Larkin got through with his 'breasts and cunt' and 'They fuck you up, your mum and dad', in a more enlightened time than today? Maybe that's why?) to publish you, I don't think so.
My life in England has been mapped out by a perverse fate to be one of total obscurity; 'Your ugly mug doesn't fit in here, fuck off', is how I'd sum it up. And not being a homicidal maniac, or cold-blooded psychopath by nature, (unlike that 16-year-old who's just been banged-up at HM's pleasure for butchering his adoring girlfriend 2-years ago, when he was only 14!, the same age as she was then), I've taken it on my substantial chin; leaving me feeling like a punch-drunk boxer whose taken a few too many blows to the head and heart.
If I hadn't decided, aged 53 (or was it 54?) to take my life in my hands and go to Thailand on my own, a daunting prospect due to my severe visual handicap, I don't know what dilapidated state I'd be in now; (I can't find 'delapidated' in any of my 4 dictionaries). I've often toyed with the idea of suicide, and horribly, ironically, (it's a parallel world out there [in Thailand] for me), women find me more attractive than the negative response I get here; and the climate suits me. I've even bought a little home out there that I can't afford to live in…yet! And I don't think my psychic stalkers 'long viewing' powers, or malicious eavesdropping; either on my thought processes or physical surroundings is as potent or effective, 6000 miles away.
My only hope, apart from wanting to be accepted by 'BLACK SPARROW BOOKS' (a hope denied, 16/2/06) in America, as one of their authors, is to live long enough to be able to get some enjoyment out of my condo in Thailand; and realistically, I could be looking at 7 years away for the Thailand dream to materialise, and quite possibly never for the American one. (This was written on 21/1/05, my condo is now in the process of being sold. 16/2/06.)
This piece is going to be buried at the end of 'GOD IS HOPE, AND HOPE SPRINGS ETERNAL, (not necessarily in my work though.) (Again no longer true, because I'm including it here in 'LONELIER THAN DEATH'.), a 306-page typed manuscript I'm transcribing onto floppy disc at Halifax Central Library, in order to give myself something to do, and break my near total social isolation; I'm a serial emotional groper of young female library assistants (we've got none working in the Access Room for People with Disabilities at the moment; I think I've scared them all off, 16/2/06), I think of myself as the Philip Larkin of Halifax Central Library, unofficial poet in residence.
So please remember, I wrote the bulk of this piece on 21,1,05, I've made these additional comments today, 16/2/06)   Phil Fletcher/Vincent Heathcliff

………………………………………………………………………………………

I sent a copy of this letter to BLACK SPARROW BOOKS early last year (2005); 'BLACK SPARROW' was originally set up to publish Charles Bukowski; the writer I've dubbed the 'Godfather' of American existentialist writing. He lived his life existentially too, (whatever that means). Maybe he was the one existentialist who 'got lucky' in the States, (because I haven't), like Camus did in France; though I think Sartre coined the word 'existentialism', but I could be wrong; and the only thing I know of Sartre's work is the 4 prophetic (for me) words: 'Hell is other people'. Maybe if I didn't go round thinking that, I wouldn't attract so much negativity in my life. But Sartre and Camus never went short of female attention, and Sartre was described as an ugly little man with glasses, so I must be absolutely hideous! :

21/1/05. Dear BLACK SPARROW BOOKS, I have been trawling your web site today, specifically the submissions section. Straightaway I've come across a major problem, you say you do not accept unsolicited manuscripts; you prefer work to be submitted to you through an agent…I haven't got an agent! Nor can I get one, as most of my work comes under the heading of 'modern poetry', and here in the UK, no-one's interested in publishing modern poetry, they don't see any money in it.
I have had to become my own agent and self publisher/publicist; I've taught myself the rudiments of self publishing and have produced very small print runs of five of my collections; I have them on floppy disc and also print-outs for four of them. What I propose to do is send you photocopies of the front and back covers of these collections, the longest one is about 70 pages and the shortest one is less than 20.
In the faint hope that you might like what you see, and write back to me in the SASE I will enclose with my submission, I'll then send you copies (one only) of any of my collections that takes your fancy. I'm not so much bothered about reaping financial reward for my Herculean labours; I am, after all, a severely handicapped person due to partial sight and other ailments, I just want some recognition and a performance tour in the States. Ha,ha,ha!
If this plea for help falls on stony ground, I haven't lost much (except all hope) in real terms; have you got any English authors (from England) on your books? Also, you could edit my work as you see fit, I'm not over-proud…..anymore! (I still will have my originals…
Your loving submittee. Mr Phil Fletcher, aka, AMYGDALA!!!!
'I am an almond-shaped rock, I am an island, and a rock feels no pain and an island never cries almond-shaped tears.'

PS. I thought 'Amygdala' was a part of the brain. That if 'tweeked', incited uncontrollable rage; it does according to 2000 AD's graphic collection: JUDGE ANDERSON, THE HOUR OF THE WOLF. According to one of my

dictionaries it means 'Almond, or almond-shaped rock'. Did you know that amygdala rhymes with Caligula? And he was a real 'nut' job wasn't he.

…………………………………………………………………………………………

FOURTH TIME UNLUCKY. 17-26/3/05.

Practically everything that could go wrong did go wrong, even down to staying out in the sun too long; thankfully not wearing anything but a close-fitting thong, needing to be scraped off the sand, still clutching my tanning oil bottle in my hand, leaving half of my skin and hair behind me; I just suffered third degree sunstroke fever, and what felt like 'bird flu'.
Luckily, I didn't lose lots of vital fluids doing lots of watery poo; I'd returned to the promised land where a little money can go a long way, after nearly a day of hellish travelling; and having just fugged-out the airplane loo after suffering the kind of stomach cramps you'd only expect to experience after waking up during abdominal surgery, for nearly six hours. Luckily, the green fumes didn't set the smoke alarm in the toilet off. I re-emerged to a stunned silence from those trapped in the nearest seats, but with true British aplomb I carried on walking back up the aisle to my seat, regardless. (I've used a bit of poetic licence there, tho' if I hadn't flushed it as soon as the toxic muck came out, the above wouldn't be too far from the truth.)
I negotiated the nightmare maze of airport bureaucracy as only a severely visually impaired person travelling alone, can do; rather nervously, passport control let me through.
I was feeling tired, sweaty, and 'blue', but my 'girlfriend' was there (with her mum) to pull me thru' to the taxi area, where a deal was quickly struck, and the 4 of us set off, (we couldn't have done it without the driver.) This should have been the start of a great holiday, but thanks to me and my big gob, it fell rather short of that description. Because I was feeling so rough in the taxi going down to P, I told her that I thought we should just be friends, she being so much younger than me; at that particular moment I couldn't figure out why she even liked me, I felt so old and ugly. Her English was good enough for her to over-understand and misinterpret me; I think I deeply upset her. Although, more accurately, her plans to 'milk' me for as much as she could get without having to sleep with me; I've now been ignominiously dumped.
I eventually found my bed, quite literally in the dark, there was no electricity in my lonely room. Feeling physically and emotionally drained, it pained me even to close my eyes and rest my thighs on the unyielding mattress. It's amazing that even when you feel totally fucked, there's a part of you that will mechanically carry on with the business of keeping body and soul alive; I

blame all my problems on my inadequate sight, but there are billions of able bodied people who are less motivated and more useless than me, so why should I keep feeling inadequate?
I'd travelled some 6000 miles to be here in 'limbo', at least that's how it felt on this unnaturally grey morning. I did my unpacking, my semi invalid health making it more arduous than it needed to be, I ached all over, and could have done with an ounce of sympathy.
To cut this saga down to a bearable size, a couple of things happened to make my situation easier, and by noon that day I had the ceiling fan whirring away and the fridge humming along dutifully, and an American breakfast inside me; but that's about as good as it got; over the next ten days the weather stayed hot and sticky. I had mixed success with some tricky transactions I had to negotiate, the nature of which now eludes me completely.

My homeward journey got off to a good start, with a taxi driver with a good heart; my paranoia levels had been on high alert after reading about an English tourist being murdered by one only 2 weeks before I arrived. I was in this cab for a two-hours and more ride, trying to hide on the left-hand side back seat, safely belted up. I was longing for the cool air conditioning of Terminal One, and I wasn't disappointed, tho' it left my 'tops' feeling cold and clammy.
Fortunately, I'd been told in advance which row my check-in desk was in, otherwise I'd have been in an inadequately sighted downward spiral of despair; nothing could have prepared me for what was eventually to come.
The first leg of the homeward journey got off to a tedious start, like I said at the beginning of this piece, I'd been feeling like I'd caught 'bird flu'; my head was all bunged-up with snot and a persistent hacking cough, and my appetite completely off. Some 7-hours later we were allowed to get off the plane.
Luckily, it's only a small airport where I had to transfer my flight, so no worries there. On the bus taking us out to our next plane I noticed these three overweight blokes, one of them of gargantuan girth; little did I suspect I would have this plebeian monster sprawled out next to me for the next 7 hours. My seat number was 10D, I was led graciously to it by an Arab steward. It was on the end of the 4-row-wide, centre aisle seats, directly in front of a wall with a TV-screen set in it, and behind which lay the aircraft kitchen and toilets.
As I plonked myself wearily down, I noticed a young Asian woman holding her well-wrapped baby in the seat next to me, staring intently at me, saying something about her mum; between my catarrh and earplugs I was feeling fairly numb. Another obliging steward fitted a cradle to the wall, but she still wasn't happy at all, neither was I, because this reduced even further my limited legroom; I thought she wanted me to move so her mum could sit there, I was happy to comply, I hated where I'd been put. Eventually she put her

motionless baby inside the cot and disappeared for a while. When she returned, she scooped her baby up as well as the rest of her stuff, and beat a hasty retreat; I think she thought she'd been hemmed in by baby-eating infidels. She was the lucky one, she escaped.

No sooner had she gone than I was made painfully aware of the presence, in the seat next to her on the other side, of the clinically/morbidly obese pleb; how he'd ever managed to confine his bulk to a single seat is a feat beyond my comprehension, because now he came sprawling over her vacated seat and spilled over into mine, I began to whine internally. His big-gutted mate was sat at the far end of the row, while the third of them had 2 seats to himself at the front of the row off to my left; naively, I asked him if he wanted to swap so he could sit with his mates, he answered in the negative.

This prime example of the common people (the great big wobbly fat man in the middle), had the gall to try 'speaking' to me; I fobbed him off with a world weary reply, tailing off into a sigh. I then closed my eyes and tried to sleep in the minute space left to me, only to be disturbed by a crèche-load of baby brats behind, venting their displeasure at air travel with ear-piercing shrieks and yells; even with ear plugs in, this was a living hell. And then some Asian patriarch began coughing in what sounded like an incurable tubercular way, putting my own phlegmy efforts to shame, unmitigated agony was the name of this particular game.

There's not a lot you can do on a plane, except watch a Tv screen, go to the loo, or eagerly await the next round of food and drink; I didn't want any of these, tho' I did manage to swallow 3 glasses of water. Not far out of Manchester, this gross specimen of humanity tried talking to me again; I felt affronted. I managed to say, 'Look mate, I don't feel like talking, I feel like shit and I just want to get off this plane, this has been the worst flight I've ever been on'. That shut him up and shortly afterwards my marathon endurance test was nearly over, apart from a further 2 hours of assorted train travel.

It was about 6.40am when I wheeled my two items of luggage thru' the NOTHING TO DECLARE' section of passport control, unmolested. My worst fears weren't realised and I wasn't stopped by an over-officious PC officer; the title deed I was carrying back with me could have caused me some problems if too many awkward questions had been asked. I could have become an object of interest to the Inland Revenue as well as the Benefits Agency. (So why am I saying this here? It's still not too late for me to get 'discovered'.)

My first train pulled out at 7.29am, I was grateful to be on it until 2 pleb 'loose cannons', a male and female, came right up the near empty compartment to sit opposite me. My mood dropped to well below zero, and

my paranoia level shot thru' the roof; luckily they got off at Picadilly Station without 'lighting up'; just to prove that rules didn't apply to them. I had an unscheduled extra 25-minute wait at Huddersfield Station due to a delayed train; I only managed to locate the buffet room moments before my delayed train pulled in.
Now, nearly two weeks on after going away, it feels as though I'd never been; I have the old ennui clinging to me like a life's-bloodsucking tick, I feel physically and emotionally sick (lassitude). The only hope I have to cling onto is that in 2 years time, I'll return to my adopted homeland, and do my best to own a rock 'n' roll bar; my final star shining. Phil Fletcher.

…………………………………………………………………………………………..

CROSSED WIRES AND LUNACY **(A loveless life in a cold climate.)**

When I go to bed at night to spend some time in the comparatively sane company of either Radio 2 or Radio 4, or even Radio Leeds,, my head's throbbing and pulsing, and the top of my scalp feels tight and sore; buzz-saws are whining in both my ears, their screeching arcing up into the roof of my skull, causing sparks to fly. I feel so stressed out I could weep for years, and the back of my neck and head is red with pain; repeatedly I tell myself over and over again, I'd be better off dead.
Because we're taught to fear death so much from an early age, we live too long, or try to. Not only are we outstripping the planet's capacity to recover itself at an ever-increasing rate, we're rapidly approaching our own species lack of capacity (and compassion, if my own sentiments are anything to go by) to cope with the ever-increasing numbers of old people who are artificially kept alive; much longer in most cases, than Nature intended; I like to use the apt expression 'coffin dodgers'.
My own father, who I despise, is a case in point; at 87-years-old, and with an ever-decreasing quality of life, he should have had the decency to die peacefully in his sleep a good seven years ago. But the State throws more and more money and perks at him, which just go into his bank account; the only consolation is, the longer he lives the more money he'll have to leave. I hope I see some of it, he's done precious little for me while he's been alive, and what little he has done has been begrudged, the old bastard. (If I'd been born fully able bodied, I would have expected to make my own way in life, but I was born with a severe visual handicap, and I feel strongly now that he's shirked his responsibilities towards me; allowing the 'state' to pick up the tab.)
In the mid-19th century, the average lifespan in the UK was 42, by which time I presume, their bodies were worn out (a bit like mine is now at 58) by

overwork and poor living conditions. Maybe they knew that living too long without any sense of purpose, is a living death; and besides, they were taught not to concern themselves overmuch with the rigours of this life, because it was all to come in the next heavenly one. What a cynical con of a poor mentality that sentiment is.
It's largely this loss of faith in an after life, (though Spiritualists believe that you 'pass over' whether you believe or not), that keeps old people creaking around on this earthly plane much longer than they otherwise might feel inclined too; and they're always pleading poverty and social neglect; the sooner this crop of dozy old coffin dodgers pops off, the better.
I'm talking about the type that keep all their money in the house (life savings etc), keep using the post office to collect their pensions because they can't cope with 'direct payment', and who let 'cowboy builders' fleece them over and over again.
Your life loses most of its credibility after 70, if my health deterioration continues at its present rate, due to a combination of a lousy climate, a loveless existence, and an inhuman share of mindless adversity, I'll be lucky if I can still bend my arthritic fingers round my long-suffering penis; my arthritis, brought on by stress, is so bad. I think that like 'the old man of the sea', too many old people in the world is choking the life out of the young, who are effectively working to keep the old fuckers going. (Of course physically, I'm one of them.)
Death has got a lot to offer for the socially redundant, and how much longer can the food chain support them? 22/4/05.

PS. I've had no contact with any of my family for nearly a year now, I don't even know if the old croaker's dead (my dad), wouldn't it be ironic if he was dead and there was some money waiting for me to collect; but the old heathen's too mean to die, unless he absolutely is forced to. 23/2/06.
(Update, I wrote to him last April to ask for my 'living legacy', around £10,000 as I estimated it; but as I had little hope of a positive response I added: 'As things are now, I hate you, and I won't even be bothering to come to your funeral', sentiments I suppose that weren't likely to endear me to him. And now, as I intend to leave the UK in December for good, it looks like the 'not going to his funeral' words could turn out to be prophetic? I could really use £10,000 right now as well. 13/7/06.)

………………………………………………………………………………………

BIG BROTHER. 4/6/05.

**If you can't get a life or a lover, watch 'BIG BROTHE'.
I must admit that as a home-aloner, and a Victor Meldrew-type
Moaner, I find the'bitching' that goes on in that goldfish bowl
Of a house, very entertaining.
The most annoying thing about BIG BROTHER is, it seems to
Come around earlier each rapidly passing year.
The gaily assorted house-mates come and go, and sink without trace,
(or should do in most cases), having had their brief fling
With notoriety and fame; the mob baying for their blood as
They're flung cruelly back out into the big wide world.
Another thing that bemuses me is, why would anyone want to
Waste 50p per call, to either vote someone out or keep someone else in?
Not only on BB, but on other reality TV shows as well,
Like Z-LIST CELEBRITY LOVE ISLAND for instance: 'You decide
Who goes' means that the gullible public pay for these no-mark zeroes
'Beanos'.**

....

NUISANCE NEIGHBOURS. 4/6/05.

**For a long time now, I've maintained that the best type of neighbours
Are NO neighbours! But I can't afford to live in splendid isolation,
So, for the last 20 years, I've moved repeatedly to escape this
All-too-common form of pest.
And each time, just when I've begun to think, 'this might be it!
Peace at last!' I'll get a blast from someone's hi-fi or car alarm, and my
Nerves go on to full alert, and I can't calm down.
Why have the fates got it in for me? Being tortured by nuisance neighbours
Is akin to death by a thousand cuts. First they drive you nuts, then the
Remover's bleed you dry.
Footballer's on £40,000 a week are able to get legal aid to fight their cause,
But anything to do with 'neighbour disputes' isn't covered by the
'Legal Fund'; I'd have to claw blood out of a stone to pay solicitor's fees,
And if I lost I'd end up down on my knees in 'Cardboard City'.**

....

MY TORTURED LIBIDO. 4/6/05.

It strikes me that along with sexual liberation for women
Has come the sad fact that many men don't get much loving
Any more. Even during the era of 'free love', I never got any;
Most members of the opposite sex viewing me as too facially challenged
To be seen out with. At times my life has been lonelier than death.
Nowadays, when I'm in the presence of a non-aggressive female,
And we're getting along politely, my tortured libido starts
Crying out for attention and affection, and I have to mentally
Beat it down with a big stick till it lies in a corner, bleeding and sick;
Because most of the women I come into contact with aren't free,
And wouldn't want to risk their staid relationships for an uncertain
Fling with me. That's what I tell myself repeatedly as I tend to my
Wounded pride, and my post-traumatic-stress-disorder-suffering sexuality.

……………………………………………………………………………………

(I wrote the above 3 short pieces for the chance to win a £1000 prize in a poetry comp' for United Press; they were judged not good enough to win a prize, but MY TORTURED LIBIDO is out there in an anthology called 'MIXED EMOTIONS', which I wouldn't touch with the proverbial 10-foot barge pole. 23/2/06.)

……………………………………………………………………………………

DISEMBOWELLED DAILY.

(There's a parallel with the Richard Kazaly story here; the young man who was ditched by his girlfriend due to his violent mood swings, and then in a hashish-fuelled rage, he attacked a young woman pushing a baby in a pram, who looked like his ex, narrowly missing killing her; then in remorse he drove up to Scotland and topped himself, he was only 23. In my younger years I've felt just as close to the edge as he did, narrowly missing plunging into the abyss.)

Just because I put on a protective front it doesn't mean I don't have feelings; behind my stern, unsmiling face lies a deep ocean of heartache in the midst of which is an island of dead dreams; a place lonelier than death, occupied by me alone. How I long to escape this place of echoes and desolation, with its vast,

dimly lit mausoleums full of monstrous corpses of memories that will attack if they're disturbed or provoked.

Well, that descriptive paragraph should send a shudder down the backs of any well-adjusted, healthy readers, taking them to areas of their subconscious that they keep well hid from themselves for good reasons; but my philosophy is: why suffer alone and in silence? If more people 'shared', the national suicide rate might be halved, especially amongst the young, who're usually among the most emotionally vulnerable in our 'first past the post', cut throat society.

I've always turned my rejections, mainly by women, publishers, and employers, in on myself; I seriously tried to commit suicide about 25 years ago because of this never-ending pattern, (this was due to being rejected by a female, the most painful cut of all); taking enough booze and pills to fell your average ox. But, obviously, fate decreed that I hadn't suffered enough, so after a nice, long, death-like sleep, lasting over 24-hours, I was left (alone again unnaturally) to pick up the pieces of my empty life.

Last year I wrote a piece called 'PLACE YOUR FAITH IN YOURSELF', it's my anthem; I paid 6 quid to enter it into a snooty poetry comp'. Needless to say it sank without trace, along with my money.

Yes, next to numerous rejections from potential women of 'my dreams', (how that snivelling, long nosed creep, Woody Allen, ever got away with the women he did, including his adopted step daughter, is a mystery to me; I'm no worse-looking than him and a lot more masculine), the most hurtful rejections have come from publishers; it's been a long and painful learning curve to get where I am now...back where I started, with my head firmly wedged up my own unsavoury-smelling arsehole. I've learned that anyone can be a 'publisher'; I've been one myself, a self-publisher. But unless you've got enough cash to advertise your product fairly aggressively, and get publicity, free or otherwise, you're fucked...so I'm fucked!

Employment-wise I'm fucked as well, now that all the adversity I've suffered has ruined my health; and anyway, who's crying out for a 58-year-old labourer with sight and arthritis and rheumatism problems? Should I try asking GOOGLE's search engine to come up with a suitable answer? I don't think so...it just might.

I do know that I love communicating, especially through the written word. Much too late now, I realise that if I'd stuck with the Labour Party when I moved to Calderdale in 1986, some 19 years ago, I might have been a councillor by now; a nice cushy number for those who like sitting around in meetings and going to conferences and junkets; the pay scale is quite attractive too. Oh well, another missed opportunity.

It's taken me about 20 days to write this short piece, I've been too full of apathy, malaise, ennui, and lassitude to deal with it. I sincerely hope and pray that this will be the last demand I make on myself to do this kind of exercise; I

feel physically and mentally spent. This will serve as the last piece (oh no it won't!) in my 'LONELIER THAN DEATH' collection. A collection that I would like to include all my diary entries into, thus making it a really thick set of volumes; perhaps to be produced posthumously by 'BLACK SUN PRESS', of which I'm the founder and editor.
('Dream on, you deluded old chump!' Founder and editor of THE BLACK SUN PRESS. 23/5/05.)

...

NIHILISTIC NARCISSISM. **(The twin flowers of evil.)**

Twin flowers of evil have been planted in my psyche, their tendril-like roots wrapping their insidious selves around my heart and soul, burrowing in like cerebral tape worms, sucking out my life's blood, becoming bloated and stinking of rot and decay, leaving me feeling lonelier than death.
My mood has picked up, along with the weather; a taste of glorious, life-giving summer is here for a no doubt, short duration, keeping the worst of the dark forces at bay. Imagine my sense of devastation and isolation lightening up after I read this extract in 'VIZ 146', earlier on. It's supposed to be light-hearted, piss-taking satire, but many a true word is spoken in jest, etc. It's part of a mock, full page ad for: 'A CENTURY OF DISASTER THROWS: BEAUTIFUL TAPESTRIES WOVEN FROM THE VERY FINEST OF CLOTHS CAPTURE EVERY DETAIL!'

THE DIANABURY MINT PRESENT...20th CENTURY DISASTER COLLECTOR THROWS'. 'Just as 9/11, the first financially marketable disaster of the 21st century, brought the people of America and Iraq together, there's nothing like a good tragedy to unite everyone in thanking fuck it wasn't ourselves. Now, for the very first time, Dianabury Mint are proud to present a timely reminder of the previous century's most famous calamities. Wallow in your very own pit of desperation and fear, whilst comforting yourself in the warmth of one of our wrap-around disaster throws, remembering all the while that you are nothing but an insignificant speck of dust on this doom-laden planet. Feel secure again instead of thinking you're just another irrelevant drone who can do SOD-ALL to influence a world that is rapidly spiralling out of control around you.
When the unexpected happens, there is nothing you can do but wrap yourself in our throws, (rocking and moaning to yourself as well, no doubt; interjection by me, PLF, drone alone.)

20th Century Disaster Collector Throws, tick here if you wish your throws to be infected with a slow-acting poison that will gradually cause your brain to erode, eventually turning it to a soggy mush'.

Of course, it's evil people who make the world a frightening and depressing place to live in; from human bombs to cold-hearted women. I've plenty of cause to fear and loathe the latter, and hopefully will never come into contact with the former. Can you imagine, the suicide bomber is brainwashed to think he or she is going straight to 'paradise'; more like 'Hell'…in pieces!!!
The only people who matter in the world today are the ones who will put their heads above the parapets and do something about the evil that is endemic in the human condition. There is a satanic desire by certain countries to start 'commercial' whale hunting again; this in the 21st century! It's as bad as hunting other species to near, or actual, extinction, when there is actually no need for any of these 'animal products' whatsoever. The whole sick industry is fuelled by ignorance, superstition, and greed.
I'm too filled with lassitude to actively tie myself to a whale to prevent it being harpooned and butchered; I can only hope that some kind of reason prevails at the International Whaling Conference. What I can do is tacitly pray for the human race to be depleted of all carnivorous and bloodthirsty elements, even though I eat meat and have a vengeful nature; I'm talking about human predators who have to satisfy their blood lust constantly. It's perfectly possible to live a full and quietly prosperous life without wreaking havoc and destruction everywhere.

If any piece of music should soothe the savage breast, it ought to be, and I make apologies for my hopeless spelling: Ravel's 'La Timbre le Cooperan, (well that's how it sounds when the snooty announcer pronounces it on Radio 3); it certainly soothed mine after yet another verbal set-too with a particularly unpleasant source of nuisance this afternoon.
Thanks to the wonders of the Internet, I've now found the correct spelling for that piece by Ravel, it's: 'Le Tambeau de Couperin', I've no idea what it means though. I wonder if it would stay a harpooner's hand if GREENPEACE was to waft this lovely, light and airy, piece of music across his ship's bows just as he was about to murder a Minkie Whale? Maybe I should write to the International Whaling Commission (a 'toothless tiger' if ever there was one) with this suggestion? Or maybe it's time those big animals (whales are mammals) learnt to use their intelligence more instead of beaching themselves in a mass suicide pact every now and then. For instance, they can dive down to great depths to hunt for squid, and stay down there for long periods, long enough to re-emerge well out of range of a harpoon gun. Why don't they even ram the boats? A pod of whales should be able to sink a

few; most whale types are too soft for their own good, they should be more like Killer Whales.

I've reached an age now where all I want to do is 'chill out'. If I could have a radio station, it would be a mix of 'easy listening' Sinatra-type stuff, the kind of low key, but worldly-wise lyrically, songs of the 30s, 40s, 50s, and 60s, interspersed with 'light music', like Ronald Binge's 'PICTURE OF A WATER MILL'; the kind of material that would calm down even the most rabid of Rottweilers (devil dogs.); the kind of radio station that Radio 2 is on a Sunday. I've no time for the dreaded 'RADIOHEAD, COLDPLAY, KEANE, EMBRACE', or any other of the death-wish-sounding merchants. And as for 'rap' and 'hip-hop'...Bleurghh! It's only the 'dance music' of the last two decades that has any saving grace for me.

It's been scientifically proven that Beethoven died from lead poisoning, largely ingested when he was a young man, as part of a regime to improve his health! He died a slow, painful death, aged 56, and if what I've gleaned is true, after a fairly tortured and unhappy life. He had a weakness for falling for piano students half his age; a bit like me in Halifax Library's Access Room for people with disabilities, falling for teenage library assistants; they're the only access I get to females, but hey! I don't mind, 'If they're big enough, they're old enough'. (I first heard that when I was impressionably young and sex-starved).

Social mores make for a squalid morass if you're over 50, having fantasies about 17 and 18-year-olds...but if things were different, or I had enough pulling power, I doubt very much if I'd look at any woman over 25 to 35, max; they become far too much like men after that, quite a lot of them in bulk, as well as attitude.

Anyway, to get back to Beethoven,, a giant of a musical composer as far as his orchestral works go, but I'm not so keen on his other stuff; I find it dull and boring, like a lot of classical music...as well as literature. Come to that, I think that every so often our cultural history should be purged, and all the 'chaff' filtered out and expunged from history; effectively consigning some creative artists to that vast dustbin forever...as if they'd never been; can U2 be put in there now please!? I heard recently that these mega rich arseholes are chasing some poor woman through the courts for 'purloined' items worth £3500; I wish a bomb would land on LIVE 8 as they are playing. I intend to watch 'WRESTLEMANIA 21' instead. Phil Fletcher, written between 19-26/6/05.

..

MY EXTRAORDINARY LIFE OF SOCIAL ISOLATION AND EMOTIONAL INSECURITY.

There's not a lot to tell really, and chronic fatigue syndrome saps what little energy I have to tell it; I merely have an annoying habit of tending to repeat myself. My story's already been told as it's gone along, in diary form and poetic song. Sylvia Plath wrote about living under a 'bell jar', cut off from everything, I know how she felt; I feel as though I'm invisible, as well as dismissible and miserable.

And yet even though I only have limited sight, my powers of observation aren't diminished; I'm far from finished when it comes to spotting a nice arse and a juicy-looking, firm pair of tits; it's the slits I have difficulty seeing (I never have) in a tight-fitting pair of jeans, (the 'camel toe'.) Women are such cunts when it comes to sexuality, talk about a duality of natural instincts! It's all to do with the morass of outdated social mores our society's still bogged down in; but compared to societies where female circumcision is still widely practiced, and the same tortured females aren't allowed out in public unless they're covered from head to foot in blue tents, with letterbox-like slits for them to look through to see where they're walking, we're positively decadent and damned to perdition.

A glaring example of the duality in women's nature's, was seen in the 'BIG BROTHER' house last Sunday night (July '05); at least that was when we got to see it. The 'housemates' (most of them hate each other) were plied with food and drink, and spirits rose accordingly. There's one guy in there who's good-looking in a very obvious way, but who's as dim as the proverbial 2-watt light bulb. One of the females, a fit-looking black nurse, has had the 'hots' for him for weeks, and there's a girl in there from Belfast who loves flashing her surgically enhanced 'threepennies' (threepenny bits is slang forTITS!). The three of them, intoxicated with liquor, ended up in the pool. The black nurse was all over Mr Dim like a rash, and just in order not to be left out, Belfast Girl let him suck the nipples on her implants. But it's the black nurse who's subsequently saying she's convinced she's pregnant; even though Mr D. swears (from what he can remember, which isn't much) that they didn't have penetrative sex; that he fingered her and she came…as well as did he…into the water! This same woman is always saying how well endowed this pleasant young man is, and he's openly admitted that the blood from his brain flows straight to his penis. All this debauched behaviour was witnessed on national TV by those of us with a voyeuristic bent….

I like watching BB because it reminds me of that play by Sartre, where 2 couples wake up in Hell, with the eventual realisation that they're going to be stuck with each other for all eternity. At least the BB contestants know they will escape eventually. What has this to do with me personally, you might well be asking? Well, my lack of physical attractiveness has led to my social

isolation and emotional insecurity; I've had more damage done to me emotionally by women than most men could endure in two lifetimes. But most of these women are too shallow to pathologically hate, they're genetically programmed to seek out the best genes for their offspring; although we're seeing more and more nowadays that they can't even do that right!!! Not that you're allowed to criticise them openly anymore, only a crazy man would do that for fear of being torn apart by the 'sisterhood'; and the darkly surreal 'PC' lobby, (political correctness.) Deriding women has become my hobby, if they won't let me fuck them, and be fawned over by them, they can FUCK OFF!

An American writer, who I inadvertently share an existential view on life with, ('a free agent in a meaningless universe'), Charles Bukowski; now dead since 1994, wrote: 'It's possible for a man to live a whole life of constant error, in a kind of numb and terrorised state, you've seen their faces, I've seen my own'. That statement, along with Sartre's: 'Hell is other people', would seem to sum by blighted existence up. Too much 'bad luck and trouble' breaks a person's health, and will, to resist the perverse whims of a vindictive fate. My health is now ruined, though I still have flashes of resistance.
Yesterday, terrorists struck four deadly blows in the heart of London, our international capital city, instantly killing 37 people, and seriously injuring nearly 100 more, altogether injuring 700. I suppose these obscene creatures regard themselves as free agents in the name of Islam, suicide bombers, torturers, decapitators, and totalitarian zealots. The dead in this situation, compared to someone who's left severely disfigured or maimed, are the lucky ones; they don't have to start rebuilding their shattered lives. But then I could be making an error in this judgement? Perhaps it all depends on your will to live, and how much love there is in your life. I recently heard of a British Army sergeant who had both his legs blown off in a bomb attack in Iraq, he was aged 30 I think, will he be able to rebuild his life successfully? (The final death toll was 56, including the bombers.)
Going back to the Bukowski quote, every morning I wake up feeling numb and empty, and terrorised at the thought of what new horrors another long, lonely day might bring. Thankfully, I can put those horrors off until 9 or 10am; I'm able to cower in bed till then. 58 years of accumulated adversity has left me with a body riddled with pain. Charles Baudelaire wrote: 'I know the Devil likes to haunt barren places, and that a hankering for murder and lust is marvellously stimulated by certain forms of solitude. But perhaps that solitariness is only dangerous for idle and aimless souls, who people it with their own passions and fantasies'.
One of my glaring errors of judgement, was to buy into a 'shared ownership' house in Todmorden; right on the cusp of Lancashire and West Yorkshire,

nearly ten years ago now. What a backward-looking, bigoted attitude, hellhole of a town that is; even in the late 20th and burgeoning 21st century's.
My biggest crime was always being on my own, hence, in the townsfolk's eyes, I was a furtive paedophile...or worse. I freely admit that my thoughts often turned to murder and lust in that barren place; it's a wonder I didn't stalk around with a lustful grimace on my face and a knife clenched between my teeth. It's only my stoic resignation to accept this 'write off' of a life as merely a phase in my incarnation cycle that has saved me from a life sentence for...
Bukowski 'got lucky' at a point in recent history when it was cool to push back the boundaries of 'good taste', to tell it like it is; not that he didn't deserve it from what I've read. He worked like a man possessed to achieve nororiety and success; I don't know if he'd make the breakthrough now, there's a paranoia about what you can and can't say in print, though you can get away with plenty of bad taste on TV.
The time IS running out for me unless I can ever afford to promote myself; my work will die with me. But hey, that's okay, there's a new Harry Potter book out next week which is liable to make its authoress a billionairess...and there's still one more of these irrelevant wastes of paper to come, for the comfortably off in our dying world to escape into, for a few hours of release from subconscious guilt, that they're contributing to the denuding of the rainforests in order to produce this garbage. Phil Fletcher. 7/7/05.

....

This is a copy of an e-mail I either did or didn't send to United Press last summer; they're a glorified vanity publisher who maintain quite a high standard of product output (they've included a couple of my pieces in anthologies, the format which I hate with a keen sense of loathing.):

'I've just read on your website that you're looking for writers with disabilities. I've had a poem accepted for your next publication, 'MIXED EMOTIONS', called 'MY TORTURED LIBIDO'. I'm not wheelchair-bound, I have a severe visual handicap and have to wear glasses with thick lenses, which have left me with a deeply ingrained inferiority complex; and judging by my lack of success with women, this complex is seemingly justified.
Writing has always acted as a safety valve for me; much of my poetic work is centred round social isolation and loneliness. I have self published small print runs of some of my collections, but I lack marketing and distribution set-ups, can you help me?' (OBVIOUSLY NOT! Phil Fletcher, the mad.)
(Update: I've now thrown most of these 'flawed' publications out, in anticipation of leaving the UK at the end of this year, 2006; they'd have been

too heavy to lug halfway across the world, and they're already obsolete, apart from becoming possible collector's items in a few years. Anyone who's interested in tracking them down should try looking for them on our local rubbish tip here in Halifax. 14/7/06.)

……………………………………………………………………………………...

NEEDLE IN A HAYSTACK.
(A title reminiscent of 'MESSAGE IN A BOTTLE' by THE POLICE.)

Realistically speaking, health-wise, even though my race is run, I still hang on in the hope that I'll acquire enough serious dough to go and have a full body scan, under a private health care plan.
I'm the kind of man who's not that far off from 60, and who could still have an optimistic outlook on life, if too much trouble and strife, hadn't irreversibly weakened my physical and mental health immune systems. I've just been reading in Baudelaire's 'La Fanfarlo' (translated by Francis Scarfe) about how too much care and woe can severely impair your 'get up and go'. I'd like to quote the whole passage here at length, but I don't think I have the strength to do so. Perhaps if I do it in stages, even though it will take me ages; I feel I must do so to put my point across that a lack of luck, love and money, are the hardest crosses to bear. (It will also help to fill my 8th, and final collection: 'LONELIER THAN DEATH', and I'll pay for copyright infringement by roasting in Hell, with a prong of the Devil's white hot, glowing pitchfork up my arsehole.):

'Well', the lady replied quite sharply. 'Dear Mr. Samuel, I am no more than a member of the public, but it suffices to say that my soul is entirely innocent. And, for me, pleasure is the easiest thing to come by. But let us, rather, talk about yourself. I'd feel happy to be thought worthy enough to read some of your own works'.
'But, Madam—is it possible that…?' the inflated vanity of the astonished bard began—'The Librarian says he has never heard of you'. She was smiling sweetly, to soften the effect of her momentary fit of teasing.
'Madam', Samuel replied solemnly, 'the real public these days is the womenfolk. Your approval will favour me with more honour than twenty academies could confer'.
'Well Sir, I count on your--, Marriette, my shawl and sunshade, please—we'll be expected home by now—you know that Master's returning early'.
She left with a gracious, if abbreviated, nod, quite uncompromising, in which dignity was not outweighed by familiarity. Samuel was in no way surprised in discovering that this old flame of his youth was now subject to the bonds of

wedlock. In the world history of sensibility, such things are bound to happen. She was now named Madame de Cosmelly, and lived in one of the most aristocratic streets in the Saint-Germain district. Next day he found her with her head bent over a flower-bed, in a graceful and almost studied pose of melancholy. He offered her his volume of OSPREYS, a collection of the kind of sonnets we all wrote and read in the days when, as Schopenhauer put it, we had short ideas and long hair.

Samuel was very curious to learn whether his OSPREYS had charmed the soul of this disconsolate beauty, and whether the croak of those obnoxious birds had spoken in his favour; but a few days later, she told him with a distressing candour and honesty, 'Sir, I am only a woman, and consequently my judgement is of little account, (try telling them that these days, ha,ha,ha! PLF); but it seems to me that the sorrows and loves of writers have little in common with those of other men. You address your, certainly, extremely elegant and exquisitely chosen compliments to ladies for whom I have sufficient regard to believe that they might feel alarmed. You celebrate the beauty of mothers in a style which must inevitably deprive you of their daughters' approval. You let the world know that you are in raptures over Mrs So-And-So's foot or hand, when, as we must suppose for the sake of her honour, she must surely spend less of her time on perusing your lines than in knitting mittens and socks for her children's hands and feet. And in remarkable contrast to all that, for some mysterious reason still unknown to me, you reserve your most mystical incense for grotesque females who read you even less than those ladies do; you swoon platonically at the feet of disreputable back-street queens, who, I suspect, at the sight of a poet's infinitely delicate person, must open their eyes as wide as cows awakening in a fire. Besides, I wonder why you are so fond of gruesome subjects, and descriptions of people's anatomies. When a man is still young and endowed with such a fine talent as yours and with all the normal reasons for happiness, it would seem to me more natural to be celebrating the health and joys of decent people, rather than condemning everything in sight and confabulating with Ospreys'.

Samuel's reply to this was, 'Madam, you should rather be sorry for me, or rather, us, as I have plenty of brothers like myself, who have been led into such falsehoods by a hatred of everybody including ourselves. It's because of our despair of ever being noble or worth a second look by any natural means, that we have painted such a strange mask on our face. We have been so intent on sophisticating our hearts, and have so abused the microscope in studying the hideous growths and shameful warts on our own faces, deliberately enlarging them, that we cannot possibly speak the same language as other men. Others live for living's sake, but to our misfortune we live only for the sake of knowledge. That's where the whole mystery lies. Age merely spoils the voice and steals teeth and hair away; but we have changed the tonality of

nature itself, we have uprooted one by one the untainted inhibitions that flourished inside our gentlemanly constitutions. We have psychologised like those madmen who only aggravate their insanity through their efforts to understand it. The years only enfeeble our organs and limbs, but we have deformed the passions themselves. Woe to the sickly fathers who begot us twisted with rickets, unwanted, predestined as we are to create nothing but stillborn works'.
'Still more of your Ospreys!' she said. 'Come on now, give me your arm, let's go and admire the flowers which Primavera fills with joy'.

And, like the old song says, 'If you want anymore you can sing it yourself', or in this case 'read it yourself!' That long dead French guy was a lot more eloquent than I ever could be, or indeed would want to be. The impetus now is to get your message across as briefly and clearly as possible; most people, apart from the annoying, professional wordsmiths, don't have the time or the inclination to search for hidden meanings, and there are far more modern means of communication available for those who do.
Of course, I'm going to contradict myself now by touching on the awful phenomenon of 'Harry Potter'. I wouldn't read any of this escapist (from reality) garbage, if all six books were presented to me by JK Rowling herself; not unless they came hand in hand with a cheque for £6 million, a million pound per book, as an inducement to read them. Now that would be what I call magic!
I can't understand how, in a world full of magical technological advances, a large and gullible section of civilised society is still convinced 'magic' can only occur by waving a wand about, or even just 'making something happen'. I've got a 7.75 inch wand that I'd like to jiggle about in a certain hot and juicy haven/heaven. I'm fairly certain it would glow in the dark and instinctively find its own way to paradise. The act of procreation, (even if you don't want to conceive), should be the only magical experience needed between two consenting adults. Phil Fletcher (and Charles Baudelaire) 31/7/05.

..

MY LAST BIG DRINK...I HOPE. (NOT REALLY.)
(Unrealistic expectations from my life.)

My TV sits in the corner of my living room, and when the gloom of a short winter's day has deteriorated into a long soulless winter's night, it's glowing light is a beacon to me in an otherwise barren universe.

I don't go out anymore, there's nowhere for someone in my unenviable situation to go, not even the pictures or a theatre show; a bloke my age, going out on his own is a social no-no; unless it's a pub with an older clientele, and even there you can feel as lonely as hell.
Living on a fixed income, and not wanting to get sucked down into a stinking marass of credit card debt, or bet beyond my means on the lottery or 'online poker', there's little choice for me but to stay in and watch TV. But I'm not complaining, penny for penny and pound for pound, it's the best value entertainment around.
Not that I don't get sick of it, and my whole socially isolated situation; I'm the longest suffering unfortunate that this nation prefers not to know about, having been forced to spend all my adult life alone; 'King of the Lonely Hearts'. Decent 'tarts' (sorry, I mean 'escorts') cost £290 for 3 hours, according to a local agency, and I don't think you're guaranteed a shag out of that! A cheaper bit of twat can be had at massage parlours (I'm led to believe.) But as soon as you've come, or run out of cash, you're back out in the cold, worrying if you've caught a nasty rash around your mouth and tongue. I've gone too long without any normal, healthy interaction between a woman and me; they're too boringly complicated for me to bother about. As soon as I get to like one of them, she disappears, or the totally inappropriate partner appears; either completely devoid of personality or 'sporting' jug-ears, (it rhymes; I was going to put: 'or having more in common with queers', but the PC gagging order has made this socially unacceptable…like me.) And the various women of my dreams can never see these glaring imperfections, reserving their judgements only for my own.
And so here I sit, growing old and more infirm, alone; and who but a super-recluse could stand this state of affairs indefinitely… stone cold sober? Not me, that's a certainty. It's not that I can't sleep without having fantasies of shagging sheep, (I'm sure I meant 'counting' the number of sheep conquests I've had), because I can; it's the sheer monotony of my life that's driven me to the comfort of the bottle and the can; but I think I've run my last race (to the liquor store) after my last big drink a few weeks ago.
If I could have died that night after my over-indulgence, I'd have died a happy man, my mind too numb with booze to have any regrets. But no such luck, I awoke to face a massive hangover that lasted 3 days, with the fug of stale cigar smoke polluting the already fetid air in my flat. Mentally, I can take these periodic lapses into alcohol's escape, but physically, my body's telling me enough is enough. It's a war of attrition I just can't win, my whole metabolism's caving in; the latest casualty being the musculature in my right thigh, and leg, coming under attack, as well as the sciatic nerve in my lower back.
What is amazing to me is, in this vast universe of ours, my whole world can encompass a radius of six feet! I sit 2 or 3 feet away from my TV, (I metre

max') with my 'remote' close to hand. If there's nothing worth watching on my 4 terrestrial channels, I'll watch a video or DVD; if I die here alone at least I'll have some company, as I rot away into my old rocking chair.
(Written between the 1st and 14th of August, 2005. And I don' really know what caused the pain down the whole of my right leg, but it was the worst and most sustained pain I've ever had; I dosed myself with aspirin and Nurofen before finally going to the doctor's, with the aid of my white stick, on loan to me from social services; and it was only after taking Co-dydromol tablets for a while that the pain subsided enough for me to discard my white stick. I hope to fuck I never have to go back to that level of infirmity again. And I haven't abused alcohol heavily since then either, not even when I went to Pattaya last December. 6/3/06. [It was my 59th birthday yesterday, no cards, no pressies, no nothing in this country of my birth; the sooner I can turn my back on it for good the better; I'd need a lot more money than I've got right now though.)
(Update, I'm going nevertheless. 14/7/06.)

...

RATS EYES. (Nihilistic hedonism, East Europeans, miserable 'indie' bands, sunsets and the northern lights.)

There's a type of human that's akin to the sewer rat in every way; it lives in filth, gorges on corruption, revels in destruction, and would probably resort to cannibalism in order to survive. I've previously described them as: 'Rats eyes in rats brains, inside human frames'....and they're scary, believe you me. They stare out from their holes, snouts and whiskers quivering, waiting for suitable prey to come along, totally toxic, and totally wrong. They do tend to come from the lowest echelons of society, but in today's culture of nihilistic hedonism, they're increasingly coming from right across the social strata. Young people committing suicide, either because they can't relate to anybody, or because they feel (wrongly) that life has got nothing to offer them, (like I heard on the radio today. A young, healthy woman took the ultimate way of opting out of life's tribulations by topping herself; the self-centred cunt, because she felt life had nothing left to offer her...well she had her 'snatch' to offer life, if nothing else.) And then there's the lowest scum of all, who overdose on heroin (and do us all a favour!) They're all guilty of committing acts of nihilistic hedonism.
The other extreme is seeing really old people, with hardly any life left in them, hobbling about; but if you tried to get near them with a lethal injection needle to put them out of their misery, they'd turn on you with a ferocity you wouldn't have thought them capable of; and batter you with their walking

sticks or zimmer frames. All this societal unpredictability is playing havoc with my mind, let alone my metabolism.
Apropos of nothing in particular, I've got the black angel of death creeping after me; it revels in my misery, 'and sure would be delighted with my company' (that's a line from JAILHOUSE ROCK by Elvis Presley), if I decided to 'top' myself; which is something I'd only do accidentally now after, say, a bout of drink and pills; (I wonder if you can overdose on St John's Wort and booze?)
I think the cult of the 'Indie' bands has got a lot to do with the suicide rate among young people, the more sensitive ones anyway; I can't stand them. 'Radiohead', 'Coldplay', 'Keene', 'Embrace', and all the rest; Morrisey's done rather well out of being professionally depressed, but I don't think he's fooling too many people nowadays, I mean, after all, you can overplay your hand can't you…even me! (I also call these purveyors of needless despair 'gratuitously miserable'; because if you're young, presentable, and able-bodied, what the hell have you got to be miserable about???)
But we don't have to worry too much now about this debilitating loss of some of the nation's young life-blood, because the EAST EUROPEANS ARE COMING!!! In ever increasing numbers, to save our sorry arses. Our minimum wage seems quite attractive to them, they can't afford the luxury of too much self introspection, they've got families to support back home. Personally, I say, 'Bring them in!' The other week in Boots (the chemists), I heard a young Russian (?) lady say 'Bazooka Gel' in that accent that makes me go weak at the knees. I would like lots more of these young ladies to come and fill the jobs that our own native stock are too full of ennui to be bothered with. I wish we could have one, full time in the Access Room in Halifax Library, unattached, and monomaniacally interested in me.
I'm fairly certain I'll never see the 'Northern Lights' now, even though you can see them up in Scotland somewhere. But certain sunsets must compare, when the evening sky is turned to red and gold, with hints of violet and soft luminous grey. I only wish my eyesight was better so I could pay greater descriptive homage to this natural phenomenon, as well as the moon and stars. But I've been sacrificed to adversity, the perversity of which, knows no bounds; it's equivalent to having 'hell hounds' on your trail that no amount of 'hot foot powder' can prevail over. (Written between 2 & 14/8/05. Phil Fletcher.)

……………………………………………………………………………………

What follows is the transcript of an e-mail I sent last year (27/8/05) to 'Reneee78@aol.com; an American existential poet, she didn't reply:

'Hi Reneee, (she did spell 'Reneee' with 3 'e's, it's not a typing error) I was trawling through the 'Poetry Webring' when I spotted your site. I've read the work on it and I identified most with the last 2 or 3 pieces on it, especially 'THE REMAINS OF THE DAY'. I too regard myself as an existential 'poet', though I'm not 100% certain that I understand the term. I've adapted a definition of 'existentialism' from a dictionary as 'a free agent in a meaningless universe'. I've self published some of my work, I could send you some if you're interested? I have a web page on www.newauthors.org.uk, or to go straight to it, tap in 'Phil Fletcher, poet' on Google's search engine. I've been turned down for publication by every publisher I've submitted work too; this is either because I'm crap, or else they find my work too controversial. I would be very grateful (as long as your opinion wasn't too existential) for your views on the work there. My saying I 'wannabe the people's poet', is meant to be tongue in cheek, (a non sensical expression if ever I heard one.) My e-mail address is philfletcher2003@yahoo.co.uk (I think we could have made dischordant music together; she looked rather fit on her website photo. Phil Fletcher. 9/3/06.)

...

And on that same day (27/8/05), I sent another e-mail to an unsuspecting punk poet, whose surname rhymes with 'pig poker'; and our relationship has deteriorated to the extent that he might physically attack me if he ever meets me, let's hope he never has that privilege:

'Hi A*** baby, is 'punk' the same as 'existentialism', or even 'nihilism'? I'm an existential/nihilistic poet: if you're for it, I'm against it; I am quite mad by the way, tho' not necessarily bad to know. I don't agree with your 'right on' views; there're two sides to every story in the news, and I support Tony Blair and George Bush in their fight against global terror. I think all you trendy lefties would be the first people Al Qaida (I hope I've spelt that fucking awful name right!) would saw the heads off. I'd hate to be at a self congratulatory gig where all you patronising bastards slag off the establishment and get PAID FOR IT!!!!!!! There are people dying in Afghanistan and Iraq so that you can keep on rocking (and mocking) in the 'free world'; you're all a pack of wankers. I didn't know when I began this e-mail that it was going to turn into a tirade; but am I dismayed? Am I fuck! If you want to sue me, good luck with it. Phil VG'. (And even after this relatively**

short space of time, I've no recollection of what 'VG' stands for. His response came a lot swifter than I'd expected, as if he was sat at the other end of the Internet waiting for people to e-mail him...which was the same case later when I e-mailed him again, along the same lines. Phil Fletcher. 9/3/06.)

....

This is a piece I wrote in response to Mr 'Pig Poker's' first email to me, I emailed a copy of it to him, and again, I was surprised at the alacrity with which he responded; I thought he might have been away doing a performance poetry tour; the old fart. I deleted his response without reading it, it might have been injurious to my fragile emotional state:

A POEM FOR YOU.

There was an old man called A***, for brains he had polyfilla.**
I heard the old bore prattling on, on Radio 4 a few weeks ago,
And I thought, 'I'm a better poet than he ever could hope to be, he just got lucky that's all'.
Now he's invited me to the vintage punk's Xmas Ball to see how hard I am;
I wonder if he wants to punch my face to the consistency of strawberry jam on
The dancefloor? Or give me a face full of dandruff? (If he's not already bald.)
Both options are a bit too rough for me; you see, I'm from the 'hippy'
Generation, 'flower power' and 'love and peace, man'. Mind you, I'm glad
That bumbling old traitor to the psychedelic movement, John Peel, is dead.
Let's hope he's being plagued in Hell by 'Napalm Death', 'Extreme Noise
Terror', 'Extreme Terror', 'The Stupids', 'Carcass', and all the rest of that
'Thrash' and 'death metal' swarm, that he sold his soul to in the '80s.
As for you, Mr A*** the Hunster, you can be the grumpy old sourpuss to**
My merry funster!
It's great innit, this poetry lark? It certainly beats scooping up dog shit in the
Park, or digging for coal in the dark. See ya...but not at one of your
Wallowing in nostalgia gigs; they're only for pigs guzzling out of the same
Trough; a person could catch more than just a nasty cough at such a venue.
LAUGHING CLOUD. 1/9/05.

..

THE POEM WITH NO AIM.

My real world hangs suspended after each episode of 'EMMERDALE' and 'CORONATION STREET' has ended; only when these imaginary lives are beamed into my living room, do I feel befriended.
I've given up trying to find some warmth to lighten up my life; I don't think it's intended. It is a jungle out there, red in tooth and claw, in the dating and mating game; if you're not awash with dosh, and above a certain age, it doesn't come highly recommended.
Online dating's okay, you can put the old hounds off your scent, and you don't have to pay a cent if you're prepared to build up 'credits' the hard and laborious way; I'd rather have a 'tart with a heart' anyway. Phil Fletcher. 26/9/05.

..

LIVING IT TOO LARGE FOR COMFORT. (Old people clinging on to life is a travesty in an overcrowded world. 29/9/05-2/10/05.)

When you're young and 'living it large', you can have no idea of the effect the ageing process is going to have on your body; and nowadays it seems that too many young people are living it too large; both for their own good and also for the long-term health of our already fractured society.
Young women are now more dissolute and reckless than young men; there are about as many of them killing themselves through too much drinking and smoking, and having unprotected sex, as there are young men committing suicide. Youth is indeed wasted on the young because their minds aren't as well developed as their bodies; it's easy to say, and think, that our society seems to be deteriorating into a cesspit of moral decay. Live for today (or the 'binge-drinking' weekend), and to Hell with the consequences....
But why should I care? This country's done its damndest to keep me down all my life, all 58 years of it. There aren't that many who would believe that a human being could stand as much social isolation as I have in a 'free society'; and still retain some kind of sanity. My main paranoid worry now is that 'the whole shit-house will go up in flames' before I can enjoy my 'declining' years. Will there be enough able-bodied young people left to ensure I get my pension paid...quite possibly in another country? Luckily, there are vast numbers of East Europeans looking for a better life, and thanks to the expansion of the European Union, we can now legally accommodate them; their young especially. And even more luckily for us, a lot of them come with much higher moral standards than ours.

About another 20 years should see me through to those mythical pearly gates. Just as our young people seem to be 'kicking over the traces' with fatal results, our older, and old people are clinging on to life more tenaciously than ever, which in an increasingly overcrowded world is a complete travesty. There's nothing nice or attractive about being old, your body aches most of the time, you can't enjoy drinking or smoking anymore, and who wants to shag old women?! Not even old men I strongly suspect; even though it's a medical fact that the vagina of an old woman can stay as fresh as that of a young one…but even so…? I myself, if ever I got lucky in that department again, would have to be careful; the 'missionary position' would be a non-starter for a kick-off, my aching back would put paid to that; not unless my much-longed-for partner was sprightly enough to put her knees behind her ears and her legs over my shoulders. I've never done it 'doggy style', or had a '69er', but I'd like to try both these positions before I die. Ideally with a consenting partner, and not with a hooker; the last sex I had was paid for, and I lay on my back and let her go on top, it was the least strenuous position to adopt for my tortured and worn-out body; (though my aches and pains ease off a bit when I'm in a hotter climate.)
There's no chance of me ever trying the 'wheelbarrow' now, not unless I wore a weightlifter's support belt, knee and elbow pads, and an oxygen mask and back pack oxygen tank. A lot of effort to go to, to see your nuts hanging out of someone's guts, and she might want pushing past her mum's house, just think what a sight that would make?
There's also a big pre-occupation in our decadent society these days with anal sex, I wonder what psychologists make of this unhealthy modern phenomenon…unless they're too busy practicing it? I have a sordid fetish about 'rimming' young ladies, I only hope my definition of 'rimming' is what I think it is. Phil Fletcher

……………………………………………………………………………………………

CYCLOPEAN EYE. 11.8.05.

I could sit and gaze at your lovely face and bask in the warmth of your rosy glow forever, but all you say is, 'You're always in my face you waste of space'. But if I'm barred from your presence, the essence of my life will be gone, the sun will have shone for the last time, and no amount of wine could blot out your memory.
Unless someone a bit better looking and more vivacious than you came along, which would suit me. A man needs to be kept constantly happy if he wants to

survive intact; in fact a ménage etroix and me were meant to be…honeys'. Phil VH Fletcher.

……………………………………………………………………………………

FERAL DESPERATION. 12.8.05.

There's a song that emphasises stark need, it's called: 'I WANNA BE YOUR DOG' by Iggy Pop; it's hard and raw, like life on the street. There's no room for hearts and flowers there, this is an urgent need born out of primal hunger and loneliness…like the kind I've suffered most of my adult life.
There could be an element of masochism involved as well in the actual craving, the need being more painfully pleasurable than any possible fulfilment; so the haunting, grinding, electric guitar riff of 'I WANNA BE YOUR DOG' could be an anthem for the eternally lost and lonely, fading into their own emptiness. Phil (Baudelaire) Fletcher.

…………………………………………………………

THE PUB AT THE END OF THE WORLD. 14.8.05.

I have a fantasy about having a Barrel Organ outside THE PUB AT THE END OF THE WORLD. One of the songs it would have on it to play would be, 'When you are in love, it's the loveliest night of the year…', which I would only play on wonderful summer, star-lit nights.
'Down At The Old Bull And Bush', would be another favourite I'd like to regale the regulars with, while my charming little monkey went round the pub, cap in hand. And we'd stay in that magic land forever and a day, a bit like Rupert in Nutwood's never changing environment.
No dues or rent to pay, only music to play, and love to be had; not bad for a-one-time mere mortal. Phil Fletcher. (And why not throw in 'You Are My Sunshine' as well? Along with 'Daisy, Daisy' ('give me your answer do…' etc.) Phil (Siano de Bergerac) Fletcher.

……………………………………………………………………………

THE NOOSE NEVER LOOSENS. 17.9.05.

I'm gazing at the full September moon through my double glazed windowpanes, I feel cut off from it, as well as the night itself. If I was out walking in a country lane with a few street lights dispersed along it, as well as some trees; I'd be able to blend the soft orange glow, the silvery moonlight reflected off the asphalt, the hedgerows and the trees, altogether with the night sky and the omnipresent full moon as the central focal point. And, if I could see better, any stars that might be visible; a living, breathing tableaux. But I've no access to such a setting, and besides, the demon car is everywhere nowadays...24-7. Phil Fletcher. (Superman 'burned'.)

....

UNPHEASANT PLUCKER. 14-18.10.05.

The more I read from Baudelaire's 'FLOWERS OF EVIL', the more I'm convinced he was a deeply, clinically depressed man...or a diabolist; not wholly unlike myself. I've been treated like a social pariah for much of my adult life, especially by women. A topic that I'm sorely fixated upon: 'Girls were made to love and kiss, and who am I to interfere with this, I'm a man, and kiss them when I can', (sung by Kenneth Mackellor I think, on a Scottish hillside, wearing full Scots regalia), runs the opening line from an old love song. My constant lament is that I've missed out on this basic need for tactile affection for far too long, and far too often; only a saint could fail to turn misogynistic (what a stupid word that is) after such prolonged maltreatment...and I ain't no saint!
If I'd had a more fulfilling life, I probably wouldn't have had much time for Baudelaire's dark and joyless outpourings, but as it is, I can relate to them, and a lot of his sentiments (or lack of them) are reflected in my own work. Here are 2 examples, translated by Francis Scarfe, whose copyright I might be infringing by quoting them here (I think he's dead now.) But hey! Who gives a fuck? (the most basic fulfilment need, after eating). Not me, seeing as I don't get any opportunity to...fuck that is; and this collection is not even going to be considered for publication: (Except in e-book form, produced by my own 'BLACK SUN PRESS'.)

DEAD BUT HAPPY. Charles Baudelaire. 1851.

In a rich soil full of snails I want to dig a deep ditch for myself, where I can stretch my old bones at leisure and sleep in oblivion like a shark in the sea.

I hate last wills and testaments, and I hate graves. Rather than beg a tear from the world, I'd prefer, still alive, to invite the crows to drink blood from every tatter of my loathsome carcass.
O worms, black cronies without eyes or ears, behold a free and happy dead man is on his way to you, you gourmet-philosophers, putrefaction's sons: wind through my ruins, then, without remorse, and tell me if there is still some other torture left for this old body, soulless and dead among the dead.

…………………………………..

THE CASK OF HATRED. Charles Baudelaire. 1851.

Hatred is the sieve of the pale Danaids. Furious Revenge with her red beefy arms in vain pours huge pails of blood and the tears of the dead into the tun's empty blackness, for the Demon drills hidden holes in it below, through which the sweats and tears of a thousand years could easily ooze away, even if Hate could revive her victims and resurrect their bodies only to crush them dry again.
Hate is the drunkard in his pot house, who feels his thirst endlessly renewed by his liquor, multiplying like the Lernaean hydra's hundred heads.
But the fortunate tipplers know when they're beaten, whereas Hate is doomed to the miserable fate of never being able to nap under the table.

…………………………………...

It's no wonder M. Baudelaire had such a severe look to him, I'm even tempted to say 'hatchet-faced'; writing morbid stuff like that. It seems that existential angst is all the rage at the moment in the poetic world, and, as usual, I'm missing out on capitalising on it. Where are all the 'slam' poetry sessions being held I want to know? Though I've developed such a deep level of low self-esteem I'd blow my chances of coming first by delivering the worst effort of the evening. I'll have to see if I can find anything on GOOGLE' s search engine; I'm only interested in winning, in selling units of modern poetry in this philistine country of mine, and it's not going to happen if I just whine, whine, whine. Phil Fletcher, whining no-hoper. 14-18.10.05.

………………………………………………………………………………………

I spoke to Alex Hall on Radio Leeds on her late night phone-in programme on 16.10.05, along the lines of: 'I can't afford a girlfriend'. I think she got a bit sick of me in the end because she seemed to cut me off. This hasn't diminished

my fondness for her battling nature; she should be made the patron saint of 'no-hopers' in her listening catchment area. I often listen in late at night, (she's on 5 nights a week between 10pm & 1pm.) This is a copy of an e-mail I sent to her the following day, and she did respond with: 'Sounds like a good self image to me, Phil'.

'Hi Alex, I'm the visually handicapped man who phoned in last Thursday night. It's difficult to articulate yourself clearly when you're live on air for the first, and probably, last time. I wanted to add that there's nothing wrong with a spot of old fashioned charm, as long as it doesn't descend into toadying…unless the price is right. (I think I mentioned on air my thwarted desire to be an escort). In my mind set I see myself as a cross between Errol Flynn, willing to whip out my rapier at a moment's notice, Clark Gable, for his charm, Robert Mitchum, for his 'cool', and Clint Eastwood, for his dangerous demeanour; throw in the singing voice of Howard Keele in his 'SEVEN BRIDES FOR SEVEN BROTHERS' role, and that's who I would like to be.
The reality is more like Keith out of Coronation Street, (Audrey Roberts current love interest), and his penny-pinching ways.
I don't know where you find the stamina to listen to all those moaning insomniacs, I'd have lost the will to live long ago; not that I don't lose it regularly already, because I do. If ever you need a flamboyant escort for the 'early bird' menu, I'm your man. I don't cost much to run. Philip. 17.10.05.

………………………………………………………………………………………

HOB GOBLINS GOBBLIN' EVERYTHING UP IN THEIR PATH, DEMONS OUT FOR A LAUGH. 21/10/05.

Light from the moon through my bedroom window takes less than 2 seconds to reach me from its source, as I lie in my bed; my head tucked into the pillow, lying on my right side, the blanket pulled up closely round my neck; I feel snug and warm. It's a misty autumn half-moon, a bright light in the night sky. It would be a cold night to be homeless, even though it's only mid-October, (not a marvellous night for a moon dance, unless you were well wrapped-up.) It comes in off the hills, a cold wind or breeze, don't ask me where the cold comes from, I'm no good at geography or meteorology.
I find my existence in Halifax a cold and lonely one, but then I've always found England a cold and lonely country for a lot of us who are born here; and now I know I'm never going to find my soul mate, my like-minded 'English Rose', who won't be merely interested in seeing if she can detect the

evil in me, which she is certain lies behind my cruel face (or else ripping my ideas off or trying to break my spirit), there's nothing left for me here except prolonged social isolation and misery.

I'm just starting to read Albert Camus 'THE OUTSIDER' again, it's been well over half my lifetime since I read it last (about 35 years ago). There's a line quoted in the 'Introduction' by Peter Dunwoodie, from an 'Afterword' by Camus to the 1955 American Edition of 'THE OUTSIDER': 'He (Meursault) is an outsider to the society in which he lives, wandering on the fringe, on the outskirts of life, solitary and sensual'; that's me here in Halifax and the whole of Calderdale; there's no room at the inn for this old boy. If being on my own didn't eat away at me like a cancer, it would be okay, a 'cool' position to be in. Most relationships are fuck-ups anyway, if what I've gleaned off the TV is anything to go by. I've never been deemed fit enough (in every sense of the word) to enjoy an adult relationship, a searing fact I'll have to take to my grave.

THE OUTSIDER seems to be a classic example of amoral, even nihilistic behaviour and attitude. The main character Meursault, just drifts along with life without any particular sentiments or emotions; he dispassionately observes his own actions; even when he kills a man he isn't particularly sorry about it, his level of ennui is too ingrained. The examining magistrate jokingly calls him: 'Mr. Anti Christ' during interviews, but the state prosecutor regards him as a heartless monster and successfully convinces the jury to bring in the guilty verdict and the death sentence…to be carried out by public decapitation; the plot is set in Algiers in the 1930s.

I'm going to quote a paragraph from near the end of the book, I feel disaffected from the mainstream of life through too many disappointments; I'm sure even now that if I had a run of really good luck, my lust for life would return:

'All through the day there was my appeal. I think I made the most of that idea. I'd calculate my assets so as to get the best return on my thoughts. I'd always assume the worst, my appeal had been dismissed. 'Well then I'll die'. Sooner than other people, obviously. But everybody knows that life isn't worth living. And when it came down to it, I wasn't unaware of the fact that it doesn't matter very much whether you die at thirty or seventy since in either case, other men and women will naturally go on living, for thousands of years even. Nothing was plainer, in fact. It was still only me who was dying, whether it was now or in twenty years time. At that point the thing that would rather upset my reasoning was that I'd feel my heart give this terrifying leap at the thought of having another twenty years to live. But I just had to stifle it by imagining what I'd be thinking in twenty years time when I'd have to face the same situation anyway. Given that you've got to die, it obviously doesn't matter exactly how or when. Therefore (and the difficult thing was not to lose

track of all the reasoning that 'therefore' implied), therefore, I had to accept that my appeal had been dismissed'. (Translated from the French by Joseph Laredo.) Phil (the spiritually dispossessed) Fletcher.

..

THE ORIGINS OF SHIT AND PISS

If there wasn't so much crap talked and written about food and drink, and so much crap eaten and drunk in the name of food and drink, I could get more enjoyment out of the fairly basic fare that a limited income means I have to live on.
I'm appalled by 'gourmet' food, what little I know about it; I mean, who could ever have first looked at a lobster and said, 'It looks edible to me; I know what I'll do, I'll plunge it, still alive, into a pan of boiling water and see what happens.' The only fish I'll eat is Tuna and the increasingly endangered Cod; I tried some tinned trout once, but nearly threw up on it, even tinned salmon makes me feel queasy.
I unashamedly like roast beef and Yorkshire pudding, our traditional Sunday lunch, but I've not had a decent Sunday lunch since I left my mother's household some 35 years ago, that's how barren my adult life has been; my mother was a good cook.
I like curry and pizza, and spaghetti bolognaise for the taste, but spicy foods only aggravate a stomach complaint I suffer from, which seems to be a combination of irritable bowel syndrome and acid reflux, and a hiatus hernia. If I could afford private health care I'd go and have myself prodded and probed and, quite possibly, cut open (stand well back from the stench), and sewn back up again.
I was prompted to write this piece after watching, on several occasions, the totally unacceptable behaviour of that super-arrogant arsehole, 'celebrity chef': Gordon Ramsey. The man who's made a fortune by turning out products which a few hours later, if the bowels are working normally, will re-emerge as SHIT! Notoriously, some years ago, a wealthy diner paid £11,000 for a bottle of 'vintage' wine in one of his eating-places. Now, no matter how good or not, as the case may be, (I've sampled wine that cost £30 a bottle and it didn't taste any different to me than £3 a bottle 'plonk'), it tasted on his palate, as soon as his bladder was full, he was going to have to go and have a PISS! Maybe he should have bottled that particular bladder-emptying and sold it on as, celebrity distilled, non-alcoholic chateau la feet.

Eating out in the UK is big business; I saw a newspaper article the other day that said £42 billion is spent annually, a phenomenal amount of money. If it was left to me they wouldn't earn a penny; the whole concept has become alien to me, eating in public, unless it's an absolute necessity. Paying silly money to impress some female on a first date, not knowing whether she's going to dump you after you've picked up the tab; which is just about bearable if you can afford the loss, except to your ego of course, is an alien concept to me.
So, on my current income, I'll have to continue to dine at home alone, and as my digestive system now seems to be ruined, the plainer the fare the better. I don't care too much about this; I eat to live, not the other way round; and the way my life is now I spend a lot of time wishing I was in the ground, providing tasty treats for worms and maggots, and rats eating my rotting brain and eyes, and atrophied genitalia and thighs. Phil (the dead soul) Fletcher. 2/11/05.

...

Here's a transcript of another e-mail I sent, this one to OFCOM on 10/11/05 about the pre-Christmas advertising blitz that's reached epidemic proportions on TV; I did receive a letter from them saying I needed to contact the Advertising Standards Agency, and me being totally paranoid about how and where they'd got my address from, I e-mailed them to find out; looking at the e-mail print out I'm holding in my hand right now, I can see that I volunteered this information to them. Am I suffering from the Mike Baldwin effect of Alzheimer's?

Subject: Christmas ads on TV:

Description: I hate ads on TV that use the word 'Christmas' in order to soften people up for this, now, totally commercialised event, 10 weeks and more before it's actually due. I would like to see a law brought in where advertisers are banned from using this term, and substitute it with Xmas!!! Christmas does not begin until 24/12/05, and lasts for 12 days afterwards. Nowadays, thanks to overkill from TV advertising, you're sick of it weeks in advance, and any Christmas spirit that you might have had is long gone. These unwanted ads make me feel more like Scrooge than I otherwise would do, and they are a blatant misuse of a religious festival. Mr Phil Fletcher.

...

THE 'PRINCE OF SENSES' WARDING OFF THE JINX OF DARKNESS. 16/11/05.

It must take tremendous courage to face each day without sight; I only have limited sight and I feel hard done to, and resentful, because of it. I know I could have had a much more fulfilling life if I'd been born with the full quota of 'the prince of senses'. I've heard that vision accounts for 95% of sensory input, instead of the pauper's 15% worth that I've been given.
As for being born deaf and blind? I'd regard that as a fate akin to death; I know people cope; Helen Keller is a famous example. But if it had been me, I'd rather have been smothered at birth, the thought of losing what sight I've got fills me with dread because then I'd lose the independence I've always 'enjoyed'.
To me, sensory input is all-important; my love of light and colour has helped to compensate for a complete lack of human love in my adult life. I'd love to live my life more in tune with nature, to have a private garden and a clear uncluttered view of the sky and surrounding country. I had this to a certain extent when I lived in Mytholmroyd, ((a village of the damned in attitude, if ever there was one), but it was a flat on a small council estate and I wasn't allowed to enjoy what should have been a pleasant existence, due to the very unsavoury attentions of the local imps and hobgoblins. I planted rose bushes, fir trees, wallflowers and daffodils. I even paid an extortionate amount of money to 'cowboys' to put up a fence in front of my flat to afford me some privacy from prying eyes, but to no avail, the 'evil eye' can see through anything…and follow you anywhere.
The evil spirits that were omnipresent there, eventually forced me out of 'mount pleasant' avenue, and have followed me ever since. I've never had the heart to go back and have a look at what havoc might have been wrought on my handiwork; I would imagine all my rose bushes were stolen and the fir trees uprooted and the fence destroyed, obliterating every trace of my existence there; and besides, it's a leg and lung-straining trek to get up there on foot.
As a long term sufferer from the unwanted, and unlooked for, attentions of extra sensory perception, I'd love to know how it works, as well as find an effective 'block' against it. Who, or whatever, is targeting me, is able to see and hear into my physical private space, as well as invade and violate my innermost thought processes; it is a truly evil entity. I've described it as an 'obscene insanity' and an 'inhuman monstrosity', (my latest description of it is as a 'perverted lump of inhuman filth'), BUT HOW DOES IT WORK!? What does it feel like when you realise you have this 'sixth sense', and that you can use it either for good or evil? And you make a conscious choice to use this perverted gift for your own evil ends? I've got former 'friends' who are

carriers of the devil's own form of schizophrenia; because even though these people have been physically barred from my immediate environment, they're still able to 'spy' on me. But because it's all going on in their own heads, they've got no actual proof that they're hearing and seeing what they think they're picking up, and as for 'probing' your mind, they've no actual proof that they're having any effect; if they're not able to communicate with me directly to glean any evidence that might reassure them, that is.
They must suffer an absolute turmoil of inner mental conflict. I regard the criminally insane activities of who, or whatever, is mind stalking me, as the unacceptable face of obsessive/ compulsive disorder, and control freakery. My 'third eye' is non-existent, my psychic abilities are about as keen as a deaf/blind person's sight and hearing; and that's fine by me, I'd rather put my faith in intuition. Phil (the prophet) Fletcher.

...

Here's a copy of an email I sent to Russell Davies, a Radio 2 presenter for one hour a week, on Sunday afternoon's between 2.30 and 3.30pm; I find the vintage 'easy listening' music he plays from the '30s up to the '60s, very relaxing. But when he featured Rod Stewart's travesty of the American Song Book last year, I felt stung into reacting, as follows:

'Hi Russell, I listen to your programme a lot on Sunday a/noons; is it just me or does Rod Stewart sound diabolically awful in his coverage of the American Song Book standards? I think his renderings are awful, lacklustre, bland, insipid, tepid, and vapid. I call his music 'PRUZAC'; it's for people who are on Prozac and who like 'lift music', (also known as 'musac'), hence 'pruzac'; a combination of 'musac' and 'prozac'. Why can't the 'standards' be forbidden territory for these latter-day 'crooners'? In Stewart's case it was his last refuge before he fell off his perch completely; (his record contract wasn't being renewed), and the 'eagle beaked' has-been has landed on his feet again, as usual. What a pity he didn't come an ALMIGHTY CROPPER!!!
Mr. Phil (the 'has been' who's never been a success) Fletcher. 19/11/05.

...

What follows is an example of my befuddled and traumatised brain working on overdrive, it's a copy of an e-mail I sent to OFCOM after I thought they'd breached my right to privacy; there are times when I wonder if I'm coming down with Alzheimer's, but I reckon if you can spell it, you haven't got it:

'Dear S*** T*****, I e-mailed 'OFCOM' last week and received a written reply today, which has come as a surprise to me, and caused alarm! I didn't give you my postal address (I did), so how did you get it? What about my identity confidentiality? Surely you have breached this? Can you please explain to me, via email, what right you have to access my postal address this way; and if you are all seeing and omnipotent, couldn't you just have passed my original email message (about C/mas Ads on TV) onto the Advertising Standards Authority? Yours bemused. Mr. P.L. Fletcher. (In retrospect, pompous twit of this parish. 16/3/06.)**

...

Copy of an email I sent to Krev Press (who no longer exist) on 19/11/05, needless to say, I have not enhanced my career prospects as of today, 17/3/06:

'Hi, do you accept submissions from writers like me? I only put together what the Americans call 'chap books', slim volumes of modern poetry and existential writing. I was recommended to you by Anthony Cropper, who I met at a Readers Day at Halifax Central Library a few weeks ago, and who told me to look for the Krev Press on the Internet. I'm a big fan of John Cooper Clarke, but I like to think my influences are my own. I could send you a copy of one of my collections: 'DEEPER THAN NOTHINGNESS' for you to look at.
There might be content in it that could be thought controversial in today's paranoid atmosphere of what you can and can't say in print...well just delete it if you ever decided to publish me. It's been so long since I looked at the contents of the work that I've forgotten the material, and I'm too depressed to keep on checking whether I'm 'PC' enough or not. I could only afford to have small print runs done of my work, so if I do send you a copy, it's cost me over 4 quid to produce it. I hope to hear from you sometime. (I did, in the negative.) Phil Fletcher.
(Update. I'm glad I haven't had to make any compromises; now I've decided to go down the electronic route to publishing it shouldn't matter so much, and I only intend to make myself contactable by e-mail, thus creating an air of mystery about myself. [To the tunes of: 'MAN OF MYSTERY' & 'THE STRANGER' by 'THE SHADOWS'.] 15/7/06.)
...

And now for something completely different in tack to the above, a copy of an e-mail I sent to Max Hochrad at The Department of Culture, Media and Sport, Commercial and Digital Broadcasting Policy Branch on 25/11/05:

'Dear Max Hochrad, thanks for your detailed letter regarding DTT (Digital Terrestrial Television), which I received today; I'm glad that the changeover to digital TV is happening at last. I'm not happy that, living in West Yorks, I'll have to wait till 2011 before I can get 'FREEVIEW' via a set-top box, I wouldn't want the 'free' satellite option, (a one-off payment of £150!). The thought of 140 TV channels appalLs me, (I could receive that many with a satellite dish and a full subscription to SKY TV), I think 30 (plus all those digital radio stations that no-one's got enough time to listen to) TV channels (that I'd get with 'FREEVIEW') is enough for anybody.
As a licence payer, I want to get the best value for my money, is there any chance of speeding the process up? I'm fairly certain that only those with severe learning difficulties will have any problems adapting to digital TV; and as for the intellectual snobs…they don't matter anyway! Yours, miffed at the delay, Phil Fletcher.

……………………………………………………………………………………

THE SLEEP PHENOMENON. 24-25/11/05.

My bed acts as my refuge as well as my living coffin; when I go to bed at night it's with a mild sense of relief, and no fright. But when I wake up in the morning there's always something dragging at my heart and soul, the murkier the weather, the more depressed I feel. This morning was a killer, I was cringing under the duvet while Melvyn Bragg and guests were banging on about 'gravitons' on Radio 4; I'm none the wiser, because I sank into a stupor while it was on; and even if I'd been fully compus mentis and all attention, I'd still have learned practically nothing, science isn't one of my strong points. Though we'd be well up shit creek without a paddle if scientists weren't prepared to push back the boundaries of ignorance and superstition on our behalf; although I wish they'd stop finding cures (too soon) for all the diseases that Nature conjures up to try and keep our numbers in check globally.
I had to drag myself out of bed at 9.45am, and grope my way towards my electric cordless kettle to make the all-important pot of tea, and put the halogen heater on so I could huddle near it. After my customary 4 rounds of bread and marmalade (TESCO'S or KWIKSAVE'S economy brand, and I never toast the bread, in order to save on the electric), and swigs of hot, sugarless tea, I felt a little bit more like my old self. Maybe that's it, my 'old

self'? I'm certainly no spring cockerel any more, and the spring in my step's rather forced and due to bouncy rubber soles and heels on my £10 boots, (they've done remarkably well, that's why I'm remarking upon them.) If the reek I make in the toilet is anything to go by (thank fuck for air freshener,NETTO's finest at 52p a canister, not 'OUST', have you seen the price of it? 'Oof! That's bad...for my pocket'), I've definitely made old bones; my dung smells like boiled horse bones. There's an ad' on TV for a rather expensive air freshener, where this woman says, 'I can't stand bad odours', I'd love to be able to lock her in my bathroom after one of my dumps, minus her air spray can, and unable to open the window. I dare say she'd have to be carried out moaning, 'I've died and gone to Hell'.

If I'm playing unwilling host to a nest of incubi and succubae that are nesting in my belly, this might account for the outlandish stench from my bowels. Last night (24/11/05), I sacrificed...again, watching the very popular 'Doc Martin' on ITV1, to watch a documentary on BBC2 called 'THE BEASTS OF SATAN', about a group of young people in Italy who, under the influence of 'death' and 'black' metal 'music', have committed a series of brutal and mindless murders; I think the case is still ongoing, though some of them have been found guilty of murder already.

The programme went on to feature 'interviews' with some of the exponents of this dark and deeply disturbing genre; outfits like 'DEICIDE', 'INFLICTION', and others whose black-hearted names I can't remember. 'SLAYER' featured a lot as chief catalysts of death and destruction, and have been blamed for at least one ritualistic 'slaying' in California; a 15-year-old 'virgin' was murdered by three devil-worshipping youths, they're now serving life sentences.

I vigorously campaigned against the late Radio One DJ, John Peel, promoting this mindless, and lyrically (unless you're a 'Satanist' with finely tuned hearing), totally inaudible garbage on his radio programme, back in the 1980s. Now he's dead, this infamous phase in his career seems to have been skimmed over, (along with him calling his wife 'the pig' back in the 1970s).

I think anyone who deliberately searches out evil, deserves all they get. Watching some of this scum last night in film footage of them on stage, made me itch for an AK47 rifle to machine gun them with, and a bulldozer to plow them into the ground; it's a truly repulsive sound they make.

One of these bubo bands is called 'CANNIBAL CORPSE, I wonder if such a creature would view cancer victim's tumours as a culinary delicacy? The way so-called gourmets drool over bull's bollocks and penises, and truffles, etc. I wonder if a cancer tumour feeds off its unwilling host-victim's corpse after it's buried, before it dies? But if its victim is cremated, then it 'fries' along with it. The newly acquired strong-stomached, Phil Fletcher.

...

A copy of an e-mail I sent to Anthony Cropper on 28th November, 2005.

'Hi Anthony, it's me, that sad case you met at the Readers Day at Halifax Library a few weeks ago; I've only just noticed your email address inside 'JACK AND SAL', who I'm thinking of taking on holiday with me to Thailand; they'll like that won't they? Especially Sal, if her front cover pose is anything to go by.
I've now finished 'A HAPPY DEATH' by Albert Camus, a novel I can heartily recommend to anyone who's suffering from a near terminal case of life weariness…it should push them right over the edge, ha, ha, ha! I've now finished my 8th and final collection: 'LONELIER THAN DEATH', in its rough form; I will eventually have to put it on my 'memory stick' or floppy disc, if my arthritic fingers will permit me…it's not as if I've got a deadline to meet.
That's the beauty of being unpublished, you can more or less regard what you do as a labour of self love, and I wouldn't appreciate harsh criticism of my work from any quarter. I leave for Thailand next Monday, so I'll miss your play on Radio 4; I wish I could write a play about my own unhappy life in the UK, and call it 'LONELIER THAN DEATH!' That should have them rolling in the aisles…shouldn't it…?
I'm going to print off this email and add it to my 'mix' or ms. For 'L.T.D', and do a bit of name dropping, using your name.
PS. I tried Krev Press, which now goes under the heading of '57 Productions', and isn't really into publishing books from what I can make out; maybe I'll try Route sometime? As long as I'm not starving in a garret for my art's sake I've no real worries, except my injured pride at not being recognised for the literary genius that I am in my chosen field; and right now it's effing freezing in it I can tell you. See you sometime, maybe. Phil Fletcher.'

My server failed to send this e-mail to: antothecroppers@fq.co.uk, this e-mail address doesn't exist, this guy doesn't like me as much as I thought he did. 28/11/05.

(I eventually ripped up my copy of 'JACK AND SAL' unread, as far as literary contacts go, I'm totally dead! But am I bovvered? Does my face look bovvered? I don't fuckin' fink so! I have my own 'Press' name, it's BLACK SUN PRESS, and if you want a literal explanation of this, it's because I regard 'black holes' as 'black suns', they absorb energy rather than radiating it; and rather than me paying DORRANCE PUBLISHING' around £3000 to 'sit' on my work in America; I mean, once you've paid them to publish your work, they've no real incentive to push it, have they, unless they're really conscientious? If I had £3000 to spare I'd be just as well off promoting my

own work through advertising and self-publishing, etc. But I haven't, and I am beginning to regard my work as a 'labour of self-love', and when I die it will die with me.......aaarrrggghhh!!! 20/3/06.)
(Update, if you're reading this as a downloaded e-book, you'll know that I transcended the winter blues to come shining through to you, I hope you like what you've read so far? Not that I give a damn, as long as I've got your 3 quid in my bank account you can...................! 17/7/06.)
....

I've entered this next piece for consideration for an anthology, under the heading of 'NATURAL BEAUTY', to be published by United Press, the glorified Vanity Publishers. But I wrote it and sent it in before C/mas last year, and it's now March 20th, and I've not heard back from them; how insulting is that, if they don't want to use it? Really insulting, that's what:

A NATURAL DUTY. 2/12/05.

It should be a natural duty
When visiting places of natural beauty,
To take all your rubbish away with you.
Hey! We even leave corpses and body parts
On mountains nowadays.
I've heard recently of a man who voluntarily
Has bagged-up all the litter left behind by walkers
On Ben Nevis, it took him two days to bring it all
Down, it must have been a real eyesore.
How can anyone who calls themselves a nature lover,
Wade through such a mess, with little more than a 'tut'
Of disgust and despair? Dropping litter in places of
Pristine natural beauty is a sign that you don't really care about
The environment you're privileged to be in. It's a sin to deface the wilds
Of Nature with human crud; if I were God I'd ban
Them for/good. Someone should do it already until the miscreants
Have learned proper respect for the world they live in.

Phil Fletcher/Black Sun.

....

In July of 2005, I wrote a very 'tongue in cheek' letter to JK Rowling, addressing it to 'somewhere in Scotland'. The letter was along the lines of 'I wouldn't read Harry Potter unless you paid me to, but could I have some money out of your obscene millions so I can pursue the cause of true art in the form of my own work, thank you very much'.
I was rather surprised to receive a reply, dated 23/12/05, just before my usual, home alone, Christmas celebrations began; it ran along the following lines (8 of them to be exact):

JK Rowling. Box 1, 44-46 Morningside Road, Edinborough EH10 4BF.

20 December 2005

Dear Mr Fletcher;

THE VOLANT TRUST (I wonder what the fuck 'volant' means?)

Thank you for your letter dated 13th July addressed to JK Rowling forwarded to this office. Many apologies for the delay in responding, your letter had got mixed in *with an enormous postbag of fan mail (*my italics) after the publication of the 6th Harry Potter book this summer
All requests for financial assistance are now passed to the Charitable Trust set up by Ms Rowling for the Trustees consideration.
Your letter has been considered by the Trustees and I am instructed by them that the request for assistance has been declined.

Yours sincerely. Fiddy Henderson, PA to JK Rowling, Trust Administrator. (I wasn't even invited to apply again at a later date when I've learned some humility, by the obscenely rich bitch's trust administrator. 21/3/06.)

……………………………………………………………………………………………

JOTTINGS, which is exactly what the next lot of bits and pieces are, the first one is dated 20/10/05:

I give good tongue action when it comes to licking envelopes…me.

Home of the brave and land of the free, you can say what you like as long as it's not about me. 19/10/05 (?)

I'd rather have colonic irrigation than chronic irritation…but only just. 19/10/05. (Right now I'm suffering with chronic irritation because Spring is in

the air and I've got unrequited spring fever; I feel like a bull elephant in must, full of hunger and lust, anything with a pulse will do. 21/3/06.)

I've not had enough sex, and even less success. 5/11/05.

Hob-goblins gobblin' everything in their path, demons out for a demonic laugh, (inspired by a particularly aggressive burst of accelerator noise last night. 22/10/05.

The origins of shit...and piss, is the origins of food and drink. (Gordon Ramsey, that arrogant arsehole, please take note), which is where the end result of his very lucrative, culinary quizine leaves the body eventually a few hours later.)
Annually I believe, from reading it in a newspaper, up to £42 billion a year is spent in this country on eating out; that's 42 billion quid's worth of shit and piss. 26/10/05.

What Not To Watch? The antidote to: What Not To Wear. 26/10/05.

I feel as guilty as hell for feeling mentally unwell; is depression a state of mind, or a chemical imbalance? Some people regard their body as a temple...I regard mine as a temple of gloom and doom; and we've all heard of low self esteem, how about low self control when it comes to filling the hole beneath my nose with food and beverages that might taste nice, but which aren't necessarily very good for me, hence my gastric and bowel problems...1/11/05.

Skunk pussy versus Skank Posse. 8/11/05.

The night sky over Halifax burned brightly with myriads of multi coloured explosions, as I sat in watching a programme about Auschwitz death camp learning to perfect its killing techniques. Over a million people were wiped out there, a feat only nearly surpassed in Rwanda 10 years ago, (and in a lot less time too, Rwanda, not Auschwitz.) 5/11/05.

'Can I put my knob in your gob'? How 'pleb' is that!? 10/11/05.

Can a love of light and colour be a good enough substitute for a lack of human love? I hope so. 13/11/05.

I've found a 'miracle' cure for £1.64p! 14/11/05. (I wonder what it was? 21/3/06.)

THE PRINCE OF SENSES WARDING OFF THE JINX OF DARKNESS. 14/11/05.

The constant emotional threat of debt and destitution; oh, and the fear of meeting an untimely and bloody end at the hands of some socially challenged brute beasts; oh, and being burgled of all my favourite possessions as well. 18/11/05.

I bought a box of Tiramisu from Kwiksave yesterday for the first time, I've been fascinated with this exotic-sounding product since Coronation St.'s Gail Platt mentioned it years ago. Based on the description on the side of the box it promised to be really appetising; my taste buds scoured it clean to savour what flavour I could out of it, but all I got was a bland sweetness with an undefined sharp edge; I won't be buying it again...22/12/05.

The way things are going I could be 69 before I have my first 69er. 23/12/05.

A certain death leading to an uncertain eternity. 1/1/06.

Most of us in the 'civilised world' are fairly cynical about 'heaven and hell' nowadays, myself definitely included. But what if your soul is destined to roast in hell for all eternity? It's the great unknowable, you won't find out until you die and your soul is whisked off, either to bask in a heavenly glow or else to roast in the fiery depths of the devil's cauldron; where the only 'people' who can hear your screams are the other souls in torment...between their own! (There's no date for this last snippet of reassuring wisdom. Phil Fletcher. 21/3/06.)

...

The next 3 short entries are copies of e-mails I've sent to the BBC, lambasting them, because I detest the licence fee and the BBC's autocratic attitude to us, the involuntary licence payers. Just because they've been there since the start of radio broadcasting in the UK, we're stuck with them because the establishment thinks the UK will fall apart if we don't have them patronising us with fiasco's like 'ROME' (BBC2 last year), that some liberal-minded producer lavished nearly £54 million of licence payer's money on; no consultation mind you...just 'take it or leave it'. Which is what I'd like to do with the 'Beeb', have it as a subscription package option...oh well:

Copy of e-mail sent to feedback@bbc.co.uk on 27/1/06.

Re, scrapping Radio 4's early morning UK 'wake-up' theme (I thank my very limited good fortune that I'm never awake at 5.30am…6.30am's bad enough.) You could replace it with Elton John doing a version of the muslim call to prayers, which would fit in nicely with the UK's anally retentive and slavish obedience to political correctness. Maybe if the BBC released the UK theme as a nostalgic CD single, it would reach a nostalgic Number1, before it's gone forever…a bit like our national identity.
PS. I've heard this week that they are releasing it as a CD single, I wonder if my suggestion had anything to do with it? 24/3/06.

……………………………………….

Copy of e-mail sent to feedback@bbc.co.uk on Sat, 4/2/06:

Seeing footage on the BBC1 6pm news last night of muslim fascist demonstrators' calling for beheadings and glorifying the 7-7 London suicide bombings, made my blood boil with anger! Why were these people being protected by the police and not being arrested? If the equally fascist BNP had been demonstrating with similar placards, they'd have been broken up! All the contact details of these muslim extremists should be noted, and they should be deported as undesirable aliens.
PS. As for the licence fee, it should be based on the ability to pay; as usual, it's the poor subsidising the rich.

Presumably to feedback@bbc.co.uk, sent on 7/2/06, though it seems a lot longer ago since then:

What I object to most about the licence fee's even bigger (anticipated) increase/s is/are, it takes no account of the ability to pay; it's another classic case of the poor subsidising the rich, along with the national lotto 'good causes' fund. As a licence payer who can only receive the four major terrestrial TV channels, I watch much more C4 and ITV1 than I do BBC2 or BBC1; I only watch the latter 2 channels for reality TV and the occasional good comedy.
But if I was a single parent mother 'living' on benefits, with a family to provide for, the last thing I'd want to be burdened with is, having to pay for a TV licence for the largely middle-class and well-to-do BBC!!! It's an imposed tax that takes no account of the ability to pay! Take that awful 'ROME' for instance, the TV 'box office' flop that cost nearly £54 million of licence payer's money to produce; you wouldn't have committed such a cavalier

action if you'd had to look for the money through private funding. Someone's head should have been on the block for that highly expensive failure, I never heard anyone say a kind or praising word about it. The BBC is an autocratic organisation that thinks it is God; whereas, apart from its radio services, it is sub-standard to ITV. I DETEST THE BBC!!!

..

I COUNT TO TEN (to the song of the same name.)

'I count to ten, then take a deep breath, and just when I think I've calmed down, the fucking bastards go and do it again!
So I count to ten, then take a deep breath...then start screaming blue murder and bloody death!'

It seems I was compelled to think this up on the 5/2/06, and it sums up what an attack of irritability feels like. Phil Fletcher, 24/3/06.

..

Towards the end of last year I was looking at a Philip Larkin website, when I spotted an ad' for DORRANCE PUBLISHING CO, a 'subsidy' publisher; I wasn't too sure what was implied by 'subsidy', so I e-mailed them, and eventually sent them a copy of DOWN IN ONE as an e-mail attachment. I've since found out that 'subsidy' is the same as what we call over here, 'joint publication' or 'author funded'. Maybe Dorrance were the first, because they claim to have been in operation for the last 80 years. There was one company that I naively applied to some years ago called The Minerva Press; they've since been closed down...I did get a glowing reader's report from them though.
Dorrance are very expensive, too expensive for my limited funds, though I would place more store in being published in America than here in the cliquish UK. But despite several entreaties from their Ray Nikolaison I don't think I'll be taking up that particular option; for £3000 (minimum), I could do a lot of self promotion over here
In her reader's review, Heather Curley, Dorrance's editorial coordinator, used the term 'broken down relic', an expression that got to me 'big time' for a little while; I'd like to meet her down a dark alley on a dark night...just to

put things right. What follows is her review and my rather stung response to it.

Reading Report for 'DOWN IN ONE' by Philip Fletcher. January 25, 2006:

'DOWN IN ONE' written by Philip Fletcher, is an entertaining collection of the author's thoughts, musings, poetry and advice. Composed in a diary format, Mr Fletcher touches on a myriad of subjects that both directly and indirectly impact his everyday experiences. Railing against his deteriorating physical health, the result of nothing more than the unrelenting march of time, the author clearly draws the distinction between a well heeled older gentleman, and a broken down relic. Naturally he aspires to the former but realises his lot as the latter (very resentfully indeed PLF). Playful fantasies regarding a nubile counter clerk at the local liquor store ('TONGUE ON THE COUNTER' PLF) and his dilemma concerning alerting her to his prurient intentions make for amusing fodder. Other topics broached run the gamut from false teeth to putrid weather and his one time affiliation with Amnesty International.
The entries are dated between July of 2001 and March of 2003, which offer the reader an expansive view of the inner workings of the author's creative mind. Quite unique in style and mature in content, the work is at times racy and titillating, but never appears to cross the line into vulgarity (I would beg to differ, PLF.) In many cases, the author is able to effectively communicate the thoughts and desires of many men of a similar age who maintain an unfortunate allegiance to decorum, thereby not meeting Mr Fletcher's standard of unvarnished truth.
Philip Fletcher's highly descriptive style of writing combined with his witty narrative approach could enhance the appeal of this literary work.

…………………………..

This is my response, sent via e-mail on 9/2/06:

'Dear Ray Nikolaison, I've enjoyed reading your reader's review for 'DOWN IN ONE', I think heather Curley's remark about drawing the distinction between a well heeled older gentleman and a broken down relic, are very pertinent. At nearly 59-years-old, impoverished and severely disabled, I genuinely fall into the broken down relic category. Also, at 59, I've never been considered worthy or suitable enough, to act as a sperm donor, (albeit in a loving relationship, which is something else I've always been excluded from), to fertilise the vastly superior eggs of the few women I've known all too briefly in my tortured life.
A woman will put up with a lot from a man, but one thing they're not prepared to take on is a combination of poverty and disability; though even

your 'half-ton' man managed to find himself a partner. The only thing that's kept me going, is my determination not to die a complete failure. Phil Fletcher. (Update, I think I used the expression: 'broken down relic' in 'DOWN IN ONE' somewhere; that must be where she picked it up from, and reading her review again just now, it didn't seem as dismissively disheartening as I'd originally thought. It just shows how our overlong, grey winters can affect my judgements: 'I am a man of constant judgmental error'. 17/7/06.)

………………………………………

After reading such a 'glowing' review, I felt compelled to re-read 'D I O' which I hadn't looked at since I self-published it in 2004. And I have to say I wasn't over-impressed with what I read; like I said in a subsequent e-mail to Ray Nikolaison, it came across to me as a 'self pitying, whining, rant', and at the very least I would need to re-edit it and tidy it up before I could re-submit it as a finished piece of work, which I can tackle when I've finished this labour of self love. I'd need to do this with all my collections, but as it looks like I'm never going to find a publisher, and my work will die with me….WHAT'S THE FUCKING POINT!?

I have asked my fat old corpse-in-waiting of a father for a 'living legacy' of £10,000, in order to use Dorrance Publishing, but the mentally and physically diseased old skinflint (he's 88 now, the rotten old bastard) has declined to have any contact with me; the sooner he's dead the better, whether I get any legacy or not. Phil Fletcher. 24/3/06. (Phew!)

……………………………………………………………………………………

The next section is centred round my entry for this year's Bridport Arts Prize for short stories and poetry, 1st prize for each winning entry is £5000; I've entered the poetry comp'. When I first received notification of the competition through the post, my initial reaction was to send it back anonymously with 'FUCK OFF' scrawled across it. But then a kind of anger came over me and I was consumed with an urge to write something that would help to push back the boundaries of 'good taste' in poetry. I have had to reign in the worst excesses of my imagination for this effort, which I wrote in one take over a couple of hours, it's called 'POETRY IS DEAD! And it's cost me £6 to enter it for this year's Bridport Arts Prize comp', closing date for entry is 30th June, 2006. I don't expect to win, very much, not because I don't have faith or confidence in what I do, but because of the stuffiness of the literary establishment in the UK; I mean, the poetry judge is called Lavinia Greenlaw

for fk's sake, and in her blurb she says: 'A poem has to thrill or disturb me, ideally both, and I want to detect how it has thrilled or disturbed its author. I like a poem to take risks and to be as imaginatively alive as they are technically disciplined. I look for attention to the minutiae of language and authenticity of experience. Reading a poem should prompt a visceral recognition of the sensation being described'. Well, I wonder what she'll make of my masterpiece? I hope she can get past the 'language' in it, in fact I hope it's such a rude awakening for her that she has an orgasm while reading it, and will subsequently change her name from Lavinia Greenlaw to Davina Bacall. Oh well, here goes, fuck all ventured, fuck all gained I suppose:**

'POETRY IS DEAD!'   3/2/06.

**'Poetry is dead', he said,
as he sank deeper into his own grey decline,
'a bit like the world, that I've been out in and used,
but which has been no friend of mine'.**

**Conventional poetry gives off a horrid reek
Of camphor and sulphor combined,
Can you imagine that insufferable odour
Seeping up your nostrils as you lay
Entwined in the arms of death?**

**With this level of unfocused anger
Inside me, I should be out 'rapping'
On the street, outside Sainsbury's or M&S,
Spitting volleys of hatred at the well heeled,
The indifferent, and the effete.**

**'Fuck off, you fucking nutter!',
some irked, wobbly-wheeled, trolley-pushing
shopper might feel stung enough to reply,
as they wrestled their overloaded cart back to their car;
to be followed by my poisonously barbed retort of,
'Fuck off and die, you cholesterol-guzzling arsehole'.**

**But of course, one doesn't go round behaving
In such an anti social manner, if one did,
One would soon find one's self on the
Receiving end of an ASBO, or a blow or two
To the head, or emotionally dead as the
Effects of the chemical cosh neutralised**

And de-activated one's tortured psyche.

Crikey! Leggo! Gerroff! Yarooh!' were my
Favourite words when I was a boy, as uttered
By the redoubtable Billy Bunter. 'I say you fellows',
He'd shriek as he was booted round the dorm
For stealing 'tuck'. Nowadays he'd be politely shown
The error of his ways, and encouraged to adopt a low fat diet.

Express any politically incorrect views in the West
Today, and you'll be pilloried with wrong-headed
Righteous indignation, or even worse; my parting shot is:
'She was only the poet's daughter, but she said she wasn't averse'.
PPPPHHHHWWWWOOOOAAAARRRR!!!!!!

Phil Fletcher/Vincent Heathcliff.

...

3,400 YEARS OF SOLITUDE. 11/2/06.

Your remains have lain undisturbed for well over 3,000 years.
The sun has passed overhead daily as it traversed the heavens
In unceasing, silent, timeless time; most of civilised human history
Has passed you by. But I doubt if you'd moan or lament,
And definitely not cry, because your brains were removed
Shortly after you died.

Plucked out of your skull through your nose,
Using an iron hook, like very lumpy, greyish-red snot.
I wonder whose fiendishly gruesome idea was that,
To turn you into a brainless dead twat? Your coffin casket's
Got more life in it than you...I wonder what they did with your poo!?
Did they shove it back up into the empty cavity inside your head,
Giving substance to that old Arab saying of, 'You've got shit for brains'?

Phil Fletcher/Amun Ra

...

The next lengthy e-mail is another nail in the coffin of my dealings with Dorrance Publishing, we did eventually get the estimate down to under $6000,

but that would have meant just 'printing to order' etc; the offer's still there for me to take up at any time, but short of a large injection of cash to my bank balance I won't be taking their offer up. There's no date for this e-mail, but I assume it wasn't so long ago; today's date is 25/3/06:

'Hi Ray, I've received and read your attachments, the estimate has come as rather a nasty shock. If I was a well heeled older gentleman it wouldn't seem so daunting, but coming under the banner of 'broken down relic', it's a bit gut-wrenching; as far as I'm concerned the whole project would be a calculated gambling risk, $9200 is a hell of a lot of money to find. The only way I could contemplate this undertaking would be by payment over 2 years by credit card payment, if it wouldn't incur any extra costs, like a credit card charge for instance.
Rather than send me a package through the mail, because I'm in no way committing myself at this moment, a monthly breakdown of payments would suffice, taking into account the exchange rate, which fluctuates all the time. As far as I'm concerned all promotional work could be done in the States, I've no faith in the UK market, and I wouldn't be able to afford the cost of shipping 500 copies of my slim volume over here from the US. I hope this e-mail is clear and concise?

PS. I've just entered a poetry comp' with a first prize of £5000, but I doubt very much if my entry will get anywhere, it's called 'POETRY IS DEAD!' and it's got swearing in it. Phil Fletcher.

...

It does have to be pointed out that, only talentless no-hopers usually have to resort to these money-grubbing outfits; I regard myself as an exception to the rule; but if I had the cash to spare I would give it a go if only to try and inject some life into my moribund literary career. (Update. I did get my idea for e-books from Dorrance Publishing, so in a way I've benefited from them at no cost to myself; which makes me feel smugly, mentally well heeled. 17/7/06.)

...

This next piece is quite long.

OF MEANNESS AND MICROBES. (Written between 24/12/05 and 19/2/06.)

Recently, I was leaving for Thailand in my usual burnt-out state, but this time I'd met someone on the Internet, I was going to meet her, it was going to be great. (That's the rhyming bit out of the way.)
After enduring more turbulence, going over India, than I was emotionally prepared for, when the plane seemed to drop about a thousand feet in less than ten seconds, we eventually arrived at Bangkok Airport; I had another two-hour car journey ahead of me to get to Pattaya; I was booked in at the SUNBEAM HOTEL, it was around 9.30pm when I checked in.
I should point out here that, being severely visually handicapped, (I can only rely on the limited vision in my left eye), makes everything doubly difficult and stressful; how people who are totally blind cope with life in general is beyond me. For a start, you're in a physical reality of permanent blackness, like being deep inside a cave without a torch, and you have to rely on other people and your sense of smell and touch for everything. They reckon that sight accounts for about 95% of sensory input, it's the 'Prince of senses'; so how deaf/blind cope with life is a miracle. To my mind, it would be like having your head trapped inside a block of concrete, I'd rather be dead; which is a bold statement to make in our current super sensitive world. I might have to be wary of militant deaf/blind activists seeking redress...with the help of their carers of course.
I did notice while I was doing my unpacking, that there was a lot of noise coming through the double glazed windows and heavy curtains from the surrounding neighbourhood; the maelstrom-like hubbub was coming into my room on the 7th floor from the 3 bars below, on the street facing my side of the hotel. They were competing with each other to see who could pump out the loudest dance music on the block.
I finally got to meet my Internet girlfriend 3 days after I arrived in Pattaya; oddly enough she worked in an Internet café inside a hotel not too far away from the hotel that I was staying in. She looked very attractive at first sight, not quite like some of the photo's she'd posted online, (I think they were taken when she was younger), but attractive nonetheless, with a paler complexion (which was to vanish a few days later) than the average Thai, and bright eyes. Virtually the first words out of her mouth was/were a hard luck story.
We met up again that same evening after she finished work at 9pm, I wanted us to dine in my hotel restaurant, it was quiet and roomy; but she took one look inside and said it would be too expensive, and dragged me off to an eatery over half-a-mile away along a dimly lit, busy thoroughfare. I expressed my displeasure vehemently, and she allowed us the luxury of a taxi-bus back

to my 'Soi' (street) afterwards. Incidentally, the cost of the meal where we went was about the same as it would have cost at the hotel.
We met next morning for breakfast at a café near my hotel, before she went to work at 11.30am; she still looked foxy, and I suggested that I give her quite a large sum of money in local currency to take the next week off work so we could get to know each other better; she did some rapid mental calculations and agreed.

My social conscience had been plaguing me, I wanted to do 'the right thing' in order to give this budding relationship my best shot, and not just be another lonely old sex tourist. Also on that Saturday morning before she went to work, I'd paid for her, me, and her 6-year-old daughter to go to an island off the mainland coast; I caused some confusion by saying it was called 'Crystal Island', whereas I think it's called 'Coral Island'.
When we met up the next morning she looked different, her complexion was darker and freckly, and she seemed fatter; maybe she wore make-up for work? I don't know. I'd expected her daughter to be shy and nervous of me, but right from the word go this most boyish-looking girl was climbing all over me; I was the one who felt shy and nervous, my morning grumpiness and resolve to do 'the right thing' were clashing.
There were a few fraught moments, both going to, and coming back from 'Paradise' Island (which seemed a bit less like paradise than the last time I was there), swapping from one boat to another. I almost crushed the toes of my right foot in one unsteady transfer, as the boat I was trying to get into banged against the side of the ferry with the motion of the waves. We got back to Pattaya about 4pm, and she wanted to go on to see my condo, which I'd told her about at the start, in order to impress her.
The complex where it's housed is a few kilometres away from central Pattaya, so we took a taxi-bus and eventually found it. I'd gone there the previous day after she'd gone to work, to sort out what I owed in maintenance and water charges; I'd left with everything paid up to date, and with receipts to prove it...all that was needed now was for an electric meter to be installed; previously I'd paid by the day for electricity.
My 'girlfriend' and her hyper-active child loved the complex, this was a step up in the world for her, and my condo was in a good position, you got all the sun on the balcony, and it was on the quiet side of the complex, facing away from the kid's play area and the pool; I'd even brought some of my belongings over the day before, clothes, CDs, in preparation for when I moved there permanently in a few years time. I suppose I must be a really shallow person because my initial attraction towards her had worn off by Sunday evening, a bit like her pale complexion. I have to say here that if I ever meet a woman with oriental features, long black hair and a European complexion,

who wants to be with me, I'll be the happiest of men; I suppose this makes me a racist.
I'd told her that she could use my condo while I wasn't there, this set off a complicated form-filling reaction, which quite quickly brought matters to a painful conclusion.
We'd arranged to meet on the Monday afternoon to do various tasks, she needed to open a bank account, I needed to change money, and there were some forms to fill in at the condo complex. It was about 3pm when we got to the reception desk at the office there. The language barrier had caused problems in the past, I thought she'd come in useful as a translator. Before long it appeared there were problems, there was always different people on reception whenever I went there, this new lot seemed unsure as to whether I'd paid up or not, despite my receipts. There was a major flurry of papers and book ledgers being sifted through, and they only talking to my girlfriend in Thai, and not to me. I was getting more and more agitated, and eventually exploded, shouting and banging my fist on the counter, along the lines off, 'WHY AREN'T YOU LISTENING TO ME!!!?'

After my outburst I walked away to a seating area, feeling upset and a bit shaken, but a few minutes later a lady came over and apologised to me; it came too late to make me feel any better, I was left feeling miserable and disillusioned. I still wasn't sure if the electric meter, which I'd paid for, was going to be installed, and my 'girlfriend' needed a form completing to allow her to use my condo and the complex while I wasn't there; and I still didn't feel any closer to this young lady who I hardly knew.
I arranged to meet her the following evening to sign the form she needed, at 9pm in the hotel foyer after she finished work Yes! despite the fact that I'd given her money to take time off, she'd gone back after only one day, and apparently that day had been some kind of local holiday; I'd been brooding about this injustice all day but I still felt obligated to do the right thing by her, her mother, who was supposed to have cancer, and her androgynous six-year-old daughter. I'd also been feeling groggy all day, a woolly feeling in my head and limbs, and a bloated feeling. I hadn't been drinking much, just a couple of Thai whisky's with ice at a bar down the street. But a few days earlier I'd had an iced coffee at a Pizza Hut and I ate all the ice cubes, which quite possibly contained a virulent stomach bug that took a little time to incubate, and there was always a smell of bad drains as you came out of the lift into the hotel foyer.
On the Monday that I'd had the bother at the Condo Complex, I'd bought some tranquillisers from a pharmacy near to my hotel to help me sleep through the nightly din coming into my room from the bars below. And to be honest I can't remember what night it was when I first lost control of my bowels and had an accident of the worst kind on my bed sheet; causing me to

rapidly get out of bed and get the sheet off before the offending stain could seep into the mattress. Luckily, I'd bought a small packet of soap powder, quite what for I also can't remember, but some of it came in very handy for washing the sheet in the bathroom sink, which I then hung over the balcony wall to dry, and crawled off dejectedly back to bed, which I'd had to remake minus the under sheet, hoping there wouldn't be a repeat performance.
When my lady friend turned up some 20 minutes late, I was feeling very irate, and my smouldering resentment spilled out when she expected me to sign her form, giving her rights that I wasn't fully aware of, and saying she was going straight home afterwards, not even stopping for a drink. I said to her, 'I'm not happy about this situation' and she looked at me, and I saw how puffy her face looked, and I also saw her mother looking out at me for an instant. I repeated that I wasn't happy about her going back to work after taking my money, which she said she'd used half of so her mother could have some cancer tests done, but I wasn't interested anymore, I just wanted to disentangle myself from this predicament. She soon got the message and tearfully left.
I wasn't feeling too happy myself and went for a bit of a wander round the immediate vicinity, no mean feat when you can hardly see where you're walking, outside of the more brightly-lit shop and bar fronts. The atmosphere around my hotel was chaotic and frantic after dark, and made a lot worse by a constant procession of four-and two-wheeled vehicles driven in a cavalier manner; I soon decided that the safest place for me was to be seated at a table at one of the bars opposite my hotel.

I genuinely didn't want to be sitting there, it defeated the whole object of my visit to Thailand this time, and not only that, the noise was deafening and the light was a garish pinky blue, and I was terrified I'd be propositioned by a really ugly bar girl whose features I'd only be able to make out in a good bright light. I ordered a small beer and ignored the friendly greetings, after which, no-one bothered me apart from a few hawkers, and I soon took my miserable carcass off back to my hotel room where I watched some Japanese examples of American wrestling before putting my poorly fitting ear plugs in, taking a tranquilliser and going to bed; the din outside never died down till around 3am, I had complained and asked to be moved to another room but nothing had come of it.
The next morning (Wednesday) I was awake before 7am and the grogginess was gone, and I decided then and there I was going to put my condo up for sale and collect my belongings from it; and furthermore I was going to walk the estimated 5 kms to get there and save on the taxi-bus fare of 150 baht each way. I set off about 7.30am along the beach road. It was a challenging walk, during which I took a wrong detour, and struggled, due to failing energy, to get back on the right route. By the time I got to the complex the sun was quite

high in the sky and quite hot, but I knew I could get a litre bottle of ice-cold water from the mini mart there for 5 baht when I got there and slake my thirst.
In my naïve state of mind, or just plain stupidity, I'd let my ex-girlfriend have the key to my studio flat so she could get a copy cut, she still had it. Luckily I was able to contact her on her mobile and explain that I needed the key to my room; she was on the back of a taxi bike somewhere and turned up quite quickly with the key; fair play to her on that score, she could have told me to eff off in Thai, and made my long, exhausting walk a waste of time.
Naturally, she wasn't looking very happy when she turned up. But I was past caring. I told her I was selling up and wanted to get my stuff out of my room; she turned on the water works while I was repacking but it didn't do any good, my mind was made up, and she eventually left to find another taxi-bike.
I spoke to a Dutch guy who runs a property-selling business from a shop inside the entrance hall in the complex, about selling and/or renting out my condo through his company, and most of the form signing was completed right there and then, but I'd have to make one final visit with my passport for the final batch of forms to sign the following day.
While I was in the complex I'd had a cholesterol-fuelled, cooked breakfast, and I felt a bit refreshed and less stiff from my earlier exertions. To get back to the main sea-front road and easy access to taxi-buses was a brisk 10-minute walk away, along the newly laid concrete road, so I set off with my belongings suspended in shoulder bags from my back (does that make sense?) About a quarter of a mile down the road there was a turn-off on my right, which I thought might act as a short cut and bring me out nearer to Pattaya.
I don't know if it was divine retribution for my caddish behaviour, but it didn't feel like a short-cut, and I eventually began to worry that my diminishing strength would give out before I could flag down a passing taxi-bus, which were non existent where I was anyway. With only minutes to spare before I collapsed in a helpless heap, I came out onto a busy road and soon picked up a bus, and the fare back to Pattaya was only 100 baht! I tried the same ploy the next day, minus the shoulder bags and after my business was completed, and ended up coming out onto a motorway-type dual carriageway; I even crossed it and started walking along the opposite side, but I couldn't figure out where it was leading too, so I darted back across the road and retraced my steps, wondering where I'd gone wrong, and eventually found myself back outside my condo complex, which I only recognised by a big overhead sign; I'd walked round in a big circle…more wasted leg work.

I'd bought some diarrhoea tablets from the pharmacy, and I wasn't drinking any more Thai whisky's with ice cubes, but the groggy, bloated feeling was back. I was having my main evening meals in the hotel restaurant about 8 or 9pm, where I was usually the only diner, and perversely, the air conditioning had a nasty habit of coming on as soon as I sat down, making the room feel as cold as Halifax Piece Hall on a murky January day. But the food and service was good (well it was some of the time; I gave up on my staple diet of 'fried beef and vegetables with rice' after the 'beef' became too tough and the vegetables too raw), and I was only drinking ice cold, plastic bottled mineral water, and I wasn't availing myself of the temptations at the bars.

That is until my last night. I'd convinced myself there would be no harm in having a few beers at the bar opposite my hotel; the diarrhoea treatment seemed to be working...I'd only had one more accident that week.

Unlike here in cold, clammy England, where I skulk around like the local pariah or 'untouchable', I'm considered to be a bit of a babe magnet out there in sunny Pattaya; it's a complete case of parallel worlds, of negative versus positive, or even...good versus evil! As I was sitting down a young lady began frantically brushing dandruff off the shoulders of my black T-shirt, I shouted that I wanted a beer and she got me one. I just wanted to sit and watch the incredible non-stop parade of pedestrian and motorised traffic that thronged up and down the street; I've never seen anything like it. But being expected to buy things I didn't want or need soon got on my nerves. I had 3 small Thai beers, and was starting to get on nicely with my young bar girl. In fact I was trying to negotiate how much it would be to take her back to my hotel room, when the thorny issue of having to pay the hotel for the privilege came up. I said I wouldn't pay the hotel because I'd already paid for my room and that was it. I gave her the money I had left on me (200 baht), and went back to my room for the last night's sleep.

The 3 small beers I'd had, had gone fairly quickly to my head and it wasn't long before I'd tired of the wrestling and went to bed, thinking that that particular bar girl could have quite easily become my concubine if my circumstances were different; like me having plenty of money and living out there full time for instance.

I was obviously dozing rather than sleeping, when I felt my insides melt and that horrible heat oozing between my legs; if I'd been asleep it would have been much worse. In hindsight I reckon the effects of the gassy beer had precipitated the dilemma I now found myself in. Apart from having to clean myself up I had to wash the sheet out again, and this time the bug was really virulent, like amoebic dysentery. My bowel evacuations were loud and smelly...and often; can you imagine how much worse I would have felt if I'd brought that young lady back to my room with me? I don't think I attempted to sleep for the rest of that night, and as soon as the pharmacy was open on Saturday morning, I was in there, rubbing my stomach to help emphasise my problem; the attractive female assistant gave me some stronger medicine to bung me up with.

After a long wait in the hotel foyer, it was time to take the transfer mini bus back to the airport; and it was then that this Scots/English animal materialised onto the bus, and didn't stop shouting about his numerous and humiliating conquests of several bar girls, for the next 2 hours. Not to me directly, I steadfastly kept looking out of the side window, with a finger stuck in my ear; but a couple in front of us copped for the full obscene rant. He seemed the type that if you'd asked him to shut up, would have bitten your nose off and stuffed it down your throat. His type is the worst advert for Brit's abroad imaginable. He didn't shut his hole up for nearly two hours in that confined space on the bus, and a lot of his ranting was to disguise the fact that he was shit-scared of flying.

The split, 14-hour flight is daunting, especially in economy class, at one point in the return journey I'd just nodded off when there was this awful shriek in my left ear; I was startled awake to realise it was this bloke in the seat across the aisle from me who'd violently sneezed, but that was it, I was back on full crash alert, and monitoring the constant procession to and from the toilet alert as well. When we landed in Manchester it was –5 degrees centigrade or celsious, whichever one is correct, but it felt hellishly cold after Thailand, and I arrived home in time to spend another Xmas and New Year on my own.

I'm now firmly convinced that my whole life is a mockery, a parody of what I desire it to be. Examples, I'd like to be published in America, the only way I can achieve this is if I pay a 'subsidy' publisher a large amount of cash, har, har, har! I've been turned down by real publishers over there. Next, I want money badly; in the space of 2 days I get two very dodgy mailings telling me I've won £15,000 between them, but it will cost me thirty quid to release these large sums of cash; (I've since had a very official-looking mail-out from Fort Lauderdale in the States, telling me I'm in line for well over £2million, all I have to do to claim it is send £20. We're warned that anyone demanding money upfront for scams like these are fraudsters.) Thirdly, I want a good life, but I can't afford to live in Thailand until I'm an old man, even if I do sell my condo and get paid for it.

And the deepest cut of all was when the love of my life fell in love with me, but deluded herself that she loved somebody else, and wouldn't leave him for me. How do I know this? Because I'm psychically aware that's why. She was pumping these love vibes into me but convincing herself it was her long term partner she loved; I bet he wondered what the hell had happened when it suddenly all went flat on him, once I began blocking her access to my emotions; I hope their sex life went back to being really flat as well.

....

(I've finished typing this major effort up today, April 1st, 'All Fools Day', every day is 'fool's day' for me here in Halifax. Phil Fletcher.)

....

There's no date for this e-mail to Alex Hall at Radio Leeds, and if my memory serves me well it wasn't sent because of difficulty in getting her e-mail address right on this particular occasion, which I obviously didn't succeed in doing. (My researcher's just come up with 25/2/06, isn't that brilliant of him?)

'Hi Alex, I listen to you a lot, I even phoned in once, saying I can't afford to have a 'girlfriend', and that women are too fussy. I've actually refined my thinking along the lines of: women should pay for the first date (at least), because 9 times out of 10 they're going to bin you off as not matching up to their idea of their ideal man. And women over 45, unless they've really looked after themselves, should resign themselves to a lonely fate, because no bloke in his right mind would want to be seen out with them, (I suppose you'll be fuming by now won't you Alex?) Unless they want to pay men like me to act as escorts at Tea Dances and on boring ship cruises?
I think you should be made the patron saint of lonely people; you might have saved quite a few lives with your positive attitude. Your patience with that Darren the other night was remarkable; I've got no time for alcoholics or heroin addicts…but I better leave it there, I wouldn't want you to tell me to 'get stuffed' and go and find somewhere else to moan to, that would really tear me apart. Even tho' I'm a few years older than you (59?), I think of you as 'Aunty Alex', I hope this does not offend. Phil Fletcher. (Lonely old fart in a bottle.)

……………………………………

I don't even know who this next e-mail wasn't sent to, it seems to be along the same line of: women are conning cunts, etc; it's not very long:

Internet dating is not for the down at heel, unless you can persuade the lady to pay for the all-important first meal, without squealing about the cost.
Did you hear about that Welsh bloke who looked like the buck-toothed one out of Mike and Bernie Winters, bedding over 350 women he's met online through LOOPYLOVE etc? They must all have been loopy to go with him, and fall for his cheap chat-up patter; he even wears 'flyaway' collars on his shirts! Maybe they all wear 1960s 'Bolero' skirts. It's all just a big fat con, I'll be glad when my libido's dead and gone. (Phil Fletcher, lonely old fart in a bottle. 25/2/06.)

…………………………………

I sent this one via 'snail mail', I haven't had a response but I'm assuming she's received it, I wrote it on 8/3/06:

Dear Patricia Hewitt. MP, (she's the Health Secretary, you know),

I'm writing to you about the awful, and increasing self-centredness, of women in general in the UK, and the corrosive and marginalizing effect this is having on men in our fractured society. Indeed, I think women regard men now as not much more than sperm donors, and that's all they want them for…their sperm…and then preferably to 'butt' out of their lives.
Two examples of female arrogance I've heard about this week are firstly, if a woman consents to sex when she's drunk, (with a grunt and a fart perhaps, [I've just added that bit]), and regrets it in the morning, she can turn round and accuse her 'partner' of 'rape'!!! Only real sluts get drunk and incapable, and there is no shortage of these in today's Britain. Indeed, more and more young women are drinking themselves to death in their bid to be as good as men. And secondly, the case yesterday of the woman turned down by the European Court of Human Rights to use embryo's fertilised by her ex-partner, vowing to fight on till she gets her own way…who's paying her legal costs? (Another aside, it's assumed that only women have a strong maternal instinct; I've had my insides ripped out of me hundreds of times because I'm not considered fit enough to be a father; who gives a toss about my paternal feelings? NOBODY! THAT'S WHO!)
Then there's 'Herceptin', at around £20,000 per course of quite possibly unsuccessful treatment for breast cancer. Women are shouting from the roof tops about their human rights to have it on the NHS; what about men with prostate, and/or testicular cancer? You don't hear much about these scary diseases and possible 'miracle' cures for them.
And then there's the vastly inflated fear of paedophiles, which I think is another deadly weapon being used in the armoury of men-hating women to further destabilise and undermine the precarious role that men now have in the UK. I know that as a man who's never been considered worthy enough to father a child due to disability, I walk a very delicate line as an unattached male in our hysterical society. Nowadays you can't even look at children without feeling tarnished.
But the idea of organised and regulated 'paid sex' in this country is still frowned upon, and seen as something dirty; again, I would suggest, by women who have regular sexual partners…of their choice of course. So the sex industry is largely uncontrolled, except by organised crime. Where is a man like me supposed to go to find relief? A massage parlour?
I think the breeding stock of this nation is not only falling apart…but growing apart! With more and more single parent families producing more and more little warped offspring, (I was going to say 'little Caliban's and Caligula's', but that would have been too biased against my own sex.) I can only say that at 59-years-old, I'm glad I'm on my way out, because I detest today's Britain.

PS. I do wholeheartedly agree that old people should pay towards the cost of keeping them alive, even though the quality of their existence is abysmal; if they want to go against nature that's their prerogative, as long as they can afford to pay for it. (Dart the old fuckers, that's what I say…as an aside, with enough elephant tranquilliser to send them comatose into that last goodnight.) And that's how I view the use of 'Herceptin'; if women have got a home they can re-mortgage, let them pay for it that way, or else go to a friendly bank for a loan; the banks are awash with dosh right now, after the latest profits reports.

PPS Do you know what a SADFAB is? 'Single And Desperate For A Baby'…and a council flat…and a black boyfriend…and state benefits…and no responsibilities. Mr Philip I. Fletcher. (A voice in the wilderness.)

………………………………………………………………………………………

I sent this letter to Tessa Jowell MP, and 'minister for culture' on 15/3/06; she's responsible for the BBC's requests to keep bumping up the TV licence fee, and so far, has always complied all too willingly; she hasn't bothered replying to me, but I did see an item on Teletext recently which said viewers are to be consulted about the licence fee; this has been done before and nothing's ever come of it:

'Dear Tessa Jowell, MP,

I've written to you in the past about the TV licence fee and my opposition to the BBC being funded largely involuntarily I suspect, by the British public. It's okay for wealthy people like you, you'll hardly miss £131.50p (the new cost of a viewing licence after April 1st), but what about the 'economically inactive' like me, and one parent families on low incomes, students, and people on benefits? Are we dutifully supposed to go to a post office each week (and a lot of sub post offices are being closed down), to queue up to buy 2 or 3 TV licence stamps? Or risk facing severe fines because we've committed the heinous crime of not having a TV licence?
You take no account of the 'ability to pay'; and being forced to pay for the BBC is another classic example of the poor subsidising the rich; a similar 'scam' to the National Lotto 'Good Causes Funds'.
How come ITV has just launched its 4th TV channel? Is it all funded by advertising alone? I personally watch a lot more ITV than the BBC, it's a lot less patronising and condescending; do you actually have the time to watch much TV? I doubt it. And yet you've just guaranteed the licence fee will stay in place for the next 10 years!!! And we all know how cash-hungry the BBC is;

look at that big TV flop: 'ROME', they poured nearly £54 million of licence payers money into it. I regard this cavalier waste of money as absolutely scandalous; someone should be roasted over hot coals for that obscenely self-indulgent act. (I've just added that last line. PLF, 4/4/06.)
I hope if the reinvigorated conservative party wins the next general election, they'll reverse your undemocratic decision. Mr Philip Fletcher. (TV Licence Payers for Justice.)

...

A '59-er' longing for a '69-er' or two. 14-15/3/06.

I spend a lot of my time worrying about how to avoid a violent and sticky end, certainly not before I've had my fair share of sex anyway, which should take me up to about age 85 with all the catching up I need to do. Maybe I'll die 'on the job', with a fanny in my gob, and my knob stuck up to my nuts in another girl's guts? A 'threesome' in other words. That would be THE way to explode into death, a sensation of prolonged ecstasy with your final breath.
Actually, feeling a fairly constant need for sex when you don't have a regular or available partner, who'll oblige you every time you get the urge, is a pest, ('sex' 'pest' geddit? 'sex pest'?)
If I analyse ('anal', geddit? I don't) myself too closely, I'll see myself as a rather pathetic, elderly joke, always on the lookout for a 'poke' that he's not going to get; a man who has no time for women anywhere near his own age. After all, apart from natural 'wear and tear', he's still a young stud, forced to 'pull his pud' rather than compromise his standards. Well, you can only have young 'trophy' women on your arm and in your bed if you can afford to pay for them. I suppose I could run up debt on my credit card with escorts, and then fashionably declare myself bankrupt; (sounds like a good idea, especially if I could get an under graduate earning her university fees; she might even end up falling for me and my laconic charm [like Robert Mitchum maybe?]...)
In fact if I wasn't such a snivelling coward, with not enough testosterone running through my veins, I would do it; at least I'd have my memories as I sink into my irreversible decline....but I'm a bit of a prude as well, it's all part of my personal hell.
I don't like feeling possessive towards women, it's a primal and pernicious urge that modern humans should have evolved out of; yet I've felt it, welling up from my guts, a hard ugly sensation, like being too masculine; I wonder if the female equivalent feels similar? They seem much more prone to overt displays of jealousy than your average guy.

I would like to be desired by sultry young women for my intellectual acumen and cosmic awareness; I've touched on areas in my work that should have their aesthetic 'G-spot's' in overdrive, and they'll be gagging for me to do them in both their sensory orifices, quite possibly not at the same time unless I stick a vibrator up their arse while I'm shagging them; if that was the case I wonder who'd come first!? (Although I bet they'll merely pick up on my racist and homophobic leanings, and ignore all the sensitive soul searching I've done over the years.)
And even today, when women are allowed to behave more like men than men, there's still a double standard in operation. The latest passion killer is that, unless you've got her consent signed in triplicate beforehand, if you have sex with a woman when she's drunk, even if she initiates it by, say, wanking herself off with a wine bottle in front of you, with her legs wide apart, moaning in ecstasy that she wants you to do her 'doggy-style' when she's hot and wet enough (phew!), she can accuse you of taking advantage of her. RAPE!' in other words, if she comes round in the morning feeling full of guilt and remorse...I ask you...?
There's still a lot to be said for seduction, seeing a woman all prim and proper, imagining what she'll be like with your cock inside her, wondering whether she wears pants or a thong? The usual masturbation fantasy material. In fact, that's it! I finally know what my sexual orientation is! I'm a wank fantasist! A hairy-palmed solipsist. This might account for why I make love to women like a woman; I've got so used to doing it for myself, I automatically adopt the two roles in the sex act...fact or fiction? YOU DECIDE!

....

I detest writers who adopt an air of aloofness, and who set themselves up above us mere mortals scrabbling about in the real world. I missed my way, I should have gone into politics; if only at a local level. I'm always writing to the Government about something or other, I've had a lot of acknowledgements from Tony Blair's office; most of the others are a bunch of ignorant bastards, the next recipient included:

`9/3/06: Dear Mr Gordon Brown MP,

I'm writing to you because I'm concerned about the vast increase in people declaring themselves bankrupt, it's become the new 'rock 'n' roll'. Social stigma doesn't come into it; people are opting for the quickest way to get out of paying their debts. To my way of thinking it's like legalising fraud.

People are running up huge credit card debts etc, which your Government is endorsing them to write off; I've seen TV adverts informing us that if you have debts of over £15,000 you can write up to 90% off, this can't be bad. I'm only concerned because as a person on a fixed income (long term Incapacity benefit), issued to me by the State, I'm not allowed the luxury of running up a massive debt, and then conveniently 'welching' on it when the noose of repayment begins to tighten a little bit. What would happen if the entire nation decided that a trillion pounds worth of debt wasn't for them, and decided to go collectively bankrupt?
You can't expect us to have any sympathy with the big banks, currently groaning under the weight of enormous profits, can you?
Like I said, if I wasn't disabled and an involuntary member of the 'economically inactive' club, (I'm 59, with no skills other than a passable grasp of the English language), I'd be out there jumping on the bandwagon of, 'Live now and don't bother to pay it back later'.
I hope you can plug this financial loophole before it's too late. Being a thrifty Scot you shouldn't have too much difficulty.

(I remember posting this letter (the original) off to Mr Brown just before Budget Day; I'm sure he'll act on my recommendations when he's ready to. 6/4/06

..

Here's a transcript I had from the ASA (Advertising Standards Authority), regarding my one-man campaign against 'Christmas Advertising' on TV:

Dear Mr Fletcher   Your complaint about Christmas Advertising.

Thank you for your recent complaint,

We have looked at the points you have raised but don't think there are sufficient grounds for ASA intervention. Advertisers are free to advertise when or how they please as long as individual advertisements comply with our codes. We can only look into complaints regarding specific campaigns rather than generic issues, and we cannot judge hypothetical situations.
Unless you object to a particular advertisement that you feel breaches the Code, then we are unable to take action.
Although we don't propose any further action, thank you all the same for taking the trouble to contact us with your concerns.

Yours sincerely.   EH, Non Broadcast Complaints Handler.

(I did e-mail this person to say I was 'hopping mad' at the ASA's response, or rather, lack of a positive one in my favour; I've since contacted our local MP for Halifax via e-mail, but it was right on the cusp of their Eater break. Being bombarded with ads for 'Christmas', 3 months before the actual event, is really galling; hopefully by October next year (2007) I'll be out of the UK and won't have to suffer this indignity anymore…'Please let me get what I want this time'…….Dear Jesus, and I might actually start to believe in your existence, and the Virgin birth. (Peals of mirthless laughter ensued.)

……………………………………………………………………………………

And now for my final letter to Tony Blair, our 'lame duck' PM, who's shot himself in the foot one too many times:

4/4/06: Dear Mr Blair MP/PM,
the idea of people being forced to work till they're 68, is ludicrous and sinister, a lot of people are ready to retire at 60, feeling quite worn out by life. This whole pensions crisis has been taken out of proportion; what do old people need lots of money for? They can't 'whoop it up' like young people, and if they qualify, they can claim Housing and Council Tax benefit. If they own their own home it's usually bought and paid for by the time they're 65, and if they choose to live abroad, which is an ever increasing trend, they can get their State pensions paid out there, and in most countries their heating costs will be a lot less than they are here.
They can't eat and drink as much as young people, and if they try to it usually results in major health problems. My own 88-year-old father, gets the best part of £200 a week thrown at him in various benefits, plus the other concessions he gets; the money just lies in his bank account accumulating interest, (I couldn't resist getting a dig in at that loathsome old bastard's expense.)
Old people love to moan about how hard done to they are, it's all they've got going for them; they're a nuisance and they live far too long. (I'm 59 by the way.)

PS. All this media debate about when you're 'going to go', is turning you into a 'lame duck' PM. If you resign, shouldn't there be a leadership contest? All this assumption that Gordon Brown is automatically going to take over is really annoying. Mr Philip Fletcher. (Knobhead.)

(If I get another acknowledgement from Number 10, it will make about 17 that I've got.)

..

I've now got only 3 more e-mails to transcribe, they're concerned with the minutiae of my life; I've always enjoyed reading about the everyday workings of the lives of creative artists (which covers writers), I find them far more interesting than high-flown ideals. The more human they are the more I like them.
The first one concerns my own personal dilemma of 'Hell is other people', mostly in my case, so-called neighbours; I've not had a decent one for 20 years, but I have been forced to move 8 times in that time period to escape nasty ones. The original of this e-mail was sent to the man heading Calderdale MBC's environmental health's pollution team: Mark Lawrance, and not 'Lawrence' as I assumed; and if I hadn't printed off a copy I wouldn't have been able to send it; I had to go to the council's offices to have the mystery explained to me:

'Dear Mr Lawrance (and not 'Lawrence' as I typed in earlier, and couldn't send this e-mail), have you now finished your investigations into Mrs/ Ms Baker's non compliance with the noise (and vibratory nuisance) abatement order? There was a lot of nuisance being caused yesterday afternoon (Mon, 3/4/06) between 4 and 7pm; she's not scheduled to be up there (above my flat) at that time, what class has she got this slot marked down for?
I've been told that the Landlord of Heritage Mews would like her to move so he can put more flats in (by Martin at No. 22). I also offered to move to No. 34 Heritage Mews (the flat next door) a few weeks ago, but I was told the flat had been let, though there's no sign of a new tenant yet; have the metal supports been removed from above that property as well yet?
Also, regarding insulation above my flat, there's been a succession of people coming and looking up into the loft area, the last one representing Armitage Construction, reckoned that there was already adequate insulation above my flat, some 400 milimetre's he said; which is 40 centimetre's, which I think he's got wrong, that would be about 16 inches wouldn't it? Mr Philip Fletcher deceased.

(As of today, 7/4/06, I've received no reply from Mr Lawrance; this now means unfortunately, that I am at war with the environmental health dept. (Followed by mad, demonic laughter that only I can hear...)

..

This next one was sent (the original) to the PBC, the Prize Bank Consortium, who led me to believe I'd been selected to win £10,000, out of the blue; and they only wanted £3.95p for me to claim it, not like the usual 20 quid that these 'scam' outfits normally demand up front. I should have known better, but when you're strapped for cash you'll clutch at any fabric of hope (but not £20's worth). They did send me a CD, and the offer of a 7-day Mediterranean holiday to be taken any time within the next 18 months at their discretion; and I think I would have incurred a booking fee for that, so I wasn't best pleased:

'Some weeks ago I was sent a document saying I'd won £10,000 from the PBC. I declined an invitation to phone an 0906 number at £1.50p a minute to get my personal claim number, and sent for one through the post. I returned the completed form along with the document, plus 2 loose 1st class stamps, plus a waiver fee of £3.95p in the form of a cheque to the address indicated; the closing date was 31/3/06. Yesterday (4/4/06), I received a load of old rubbish through the post from the PBC…but no cheque for £10,000! Where is my money, and why are companies like yours allowed to act as parasites, feeding off vulnerable people like me, to whom £10,000 would mean a hell of a lot? Personally, I think you should be taken out and shot…very slowly. You've caused me a great deal of disappointment, I intend contacting Trading Standards about you, sending them a copy of my 'winning' document; with a bit of luck they'll close you down. Mr Philip Fletcher.' (Loser of this parish.)

(Of course, I forgot to photocopy the incriminating document but they don't know that do they?)

……………………………………………………………………………………

And this is a transcription of an e-mail I've sent this afternoon to the duty office at ITV.com; I think it's been sent, I'll have to check when I've finished today's word processing session at the library. I can't think of a better note to finish on, slagging someone with no real talent off, namely 'Jordan', the big-titted (surgically enhanced) plebistocrat:

'A few weeks ago I saw 'Jordan' on 'Davina' (on her chat show on BBC1), for a couple of minutes, that's as long as I can stand Jordan for at any one time; she, Jordan, said she was sick of only getting nice criticism for her book, the second volume of her 'autobiography'; she's only about 26, and has spent half of that time on her back with her legs in the air. Anyway, she said she wanted some harsher, 'bad' criticism for a change of her talents, so here goes.
I did read a brilliantly barbed review in The Daily Mail some weeks ago of Katie's book (J's real name), but it was so subtle it would have gone right over

Jordan's big fat head. She's part of the new 'Plebistocracy', (that's my own creation that one), her and Jade Goody are its Queens, ('Ere, leave it aht, your 'avin' a larf, incha'?). My critical opinion of Jordan, aka Katie Price, is that she's a boring, talentless slag, with about as much sex appeal as a toothless-headed hag. I intend to reproduce this e-mail in my own book of modern poetry and acerbic observations on life. But unlike her number one best seller (in *FUCKING HARDBACK AS WELL*!!!), mine will probably never see the light of day; so she won't be able to sue me will she, the gormless cow. It's no wonder her and Peter Andre get on so well together, they're as thick as each other! No more Mista Nice Guy. Phil Fletcher.'

...

RUTTING. 4-5/4/06.

I'm an old bull who's been effectively emasculated
By the social mores of today's screwed-up society.
But I can still bellow and stamp my hoof, and my
Testosterone level can go through the roof
When the human version of the rutting season kicks in…it's Spring again!

Actually, it's all in my head,
I'm feeling more than half-dead;
I'd be better off with a good book instead,
Tucked-up in bed with a hot-water-bottle
Beneath my aching back, that Fiery Jack's too smelly;
And another one on top of my belly to quell
The raging storm of irritable bowel syndrome within.

I used to have only one chin, now I've got two-and-a-half;
If I still had a hearth I'd put my feet up in front of it
And gaze into the flames, hoping to see a beautiful 'Phoenix'
Rising from the ashes, with a pale complexion and dark eyelashes,
And with no clothes on.

There we go, I've gone again,
Wandering off down memory lane,
Fantasising about when 'making love' didn't involve
Physical pain, and where I'd never end up saying,
'I'm sorry I came too soon'.

Now you can hear me howling at the moon with my terminal
Libido clutched limply in my hand, and, 'This is my very last swan song'
Etched in the sand, inscribed with my drooping penis.

Phil Fletcher, the literarily deceased.

And that's it, I'd rather have my hands and head chopped off than create any more work that no-one's going to read. I just have five pieces to add, which have appeared in some of my previous seven collections; because they're work that I think any 'poet' could be proud of. I am toying with the idea of setting up my own e-book web site under the BLACK SUN PRESS heading; all I have to do is re-edit the other work, create a web site, possibly with some help; and make sure people can't download me for free, tee, hee, hee!

...

A SUBURBAN ROAD. ('Residential Cul de Sac, actually'.)

There's a circle of stone ground outside my flat,
I'd like to be able to dance on that;
After downing a few tubes of a beer that bites,
On warm summer, moonlit nights,
And have a few women friends around.

I'd like to do an impromptu war dance to the
Compelling bass-line on 'CREAM's 'SUNSHINE OF YOUR LOVE',
Blaring out from speakers turned-up full blast,
And then imagine myself to be a green wizard to
'JETHRO TULL's 'LIVING IN THE PAST'.

But my all-seeing, all knowing neighbours, who never sleep,
And pray the Devil my soul to keep, and who know
What it takes to put me in a psychotic frenzy,
Don't take very kindly to 'SCOTT MACKENZIE' and his:
'I'M JUST SITTIN' WATCHIN' FLOWERS IN THE RAIN...'
Oh, I'm sorry, that's the wrong refrain.

'I CAN HEAR THE GRASS GROW' would have them feeling really low,
And they'd become united in getting a petition up to have me put out,
Especially if, one sunny dawning, around 4am, I decided to wake them

Up with 'LULU's version of 'SHOUT!' ('You know you make me want to'.)

**My suburban road has become my personal hell,
With fear and loathing, the normal smell.
I've planted rose bushes, fir trees, and daffodils,
And across from my windows you can see the hills.
When I moved in I had such high hopes,
But it looks as if I'm surrounded by vicious dopes.**

**Anything to do with loud cars and dogs, and their attendant mess,
Is greeted with an unspoken communal 'Yes. Let's use this pleasant
Little cul-de-sac as our own personal racing track,
And do screeching 'wheelies' in the turning circle, and squash that nutter's
Fairy ring; we'll show him that round here obnoxiousness is King!'**

**So, five years on, I'm a nervous wreck, reluctant to face each gruelling day,
Cringing behind my closed curtains, hoping the worst demon of them all
Won't come and play, 'Hunt the weirdo', and hiss at me to play 'MISTY'
For her, like in that Clint Eastwood movie.
I can't see well enough to go out and bop her one,
I'm not my hot-blooded father's son,
I have a nervous stomach you know.... Phil ('SPIRIT IN THE SKY')
Fletcher. 1992.**

...

PRIVATE FEARS. (He's the universal soldier, he's depraved and he could come and kick down your door and torture you to death at any time in the future.)

**Every time one of those stupid low-flying Jet's comes roaring
Through my privacy, jarring my already overwrought nervous system,
I don't think, 'There goes one of our brave lads, protecting me', no,
I think, 'Imagine if one of those fiendish bastard s.o.b's was carrying
His payload to drop over here?'
I wonder what it must have felt like in Baghdad or Yugoslavia
When one of these great cowards comes rushing overhead,
With its bowels spewing out destruction and death, misery and maimings?
If the Devil was born without a pair of horns it's in the guise
Of modern warfare, or the even more hideous persona that stalks
The earth and allows it to happen.**

There's nothing worse than having your daily routine's disrupted;
It's bad enough when they turn the water off for a couple of hours,
Or if there's a power cut, resulting in instant isolation and helplessness.
What must it be like when your whole neighbourhood's been left nothing
more than smouldering rubble? Of course, we all know it could
Never happen here, Northern Ireland perhaps, but never here.
And yet every time one of these monsters of the techno' age comes screeching
Through my privacy...I wonder what it must be like? If you survive their
horrifying visit that is.

And naturally it's only in undeveloped parts of the world, like Central
America (Nicaragua), parts of Africa and Asia, where human life
Is still held amazingly cheap, and unbelievable atrocities are carried out
On a daily basis. Maybe the Northern Irish death squads and bombers do
their basic training in Iraq or El Salvador?
It's absolutely inconceivable that you are ever likely to see your family
Murdered in front of you in this country, or 'disappeared'
In the middle of the night. Nor could the hills around Calderdale
Ever play host to hordes of starving and dying refugees at this time of year;
(January),presumably the D.O.E. would never permit it?

No gas for your gas fire, no water for your dish-washer,
No petrol, or road, for your life-saving car? Unthinkable!
There'll always be an England, and that good old Dunkirque spirit
Can be dragged out and dusted off anytime we need it...
Mind you, it's awe-inspiring the way supermarket shelves can empty
As soon as there's a hint of any food shortage.
Was J.F.K. bumped off by the Mafia? Sorry, I meant 'organised crime'?
Will the new Russian Commonwealth disintegrate into fascist anarchy?
With enough nuclear hardware between them to make Earth the next
Nearest smoking ruin to the Sun?
Will I die before they've screened the very last episode of 'Coronation Street'?
Oh, Holy of holies, I hope not.   Phil Fletcher. 1992.

..

MOMENTS OF CLARITY. (For Vincent van Gogh and me.)

The death of hope, and the birth of dull acceptance
That I can't find love; or even worse, that I am to be denied it.
Better to be born any other creature than human,
Rather than endure this evil fate.
To be here once in all eternity and experience
Every other emotion than the deepest one there is…….!

Better to be born a creature purely in tune with the elements,
And whose main concern is to procreate before dying,
Than suffer the pangs of unfathomable, cruel, continuous rejections.
I'd rather be a lone male tiger with merciless teeth and claws,
A beautifully developed mixture of appetite and indolence,
To eat for as long as I'm able to hunt, and to drink, only water
And blood.

As for loving? That would be controlled by a hierarchical status,
During a fixed mating season; or whether I could nip in quick
And take advantage of some randy female while the local stud
Was otherwise engaged. I wouldn't be aware that the planet is in danger
Of frying, or that my species is being wiped out to feed
Ignorance and superstition, I'd just prowl about beneath a forest moon,
And swipe at glinting stars in forest pools. Phil Fletcher. Mid 1990s.

……………………………………………………………………………..

LONELINESS

I sit on the pavement beneath the all night, all bright neon sign
That advertises the closed laundrette; its beautiful fluorescent colours
Attract me like a moth to a flame.
I've been walking dimly lit streets for hours, looking for a tavern
Where I might hear the strains of 'THOSE WERE THE DAYS'
Drifting out the door; instead all I've sensed is an atmosphere of
Quiet unease; a combination of fear from urban terrorism, plague blight,
And political correctness.

I contemplate the early dawn light, and feel myself crying, and dying
Inside, this is as far as I intend to go; soon I'll lie on the pavement and

Hopefully, sob myself to sleep; the cavalcade of insane motorists isn't due
To start up again for a couple of hours yet.
Stretching out on the glowing sidewalk, I imagine myself to be on a
Mortuary slab, the cold seeps into my head and body. A thought
Crosses my mind, or rather, a question: 'Was I born just to die alone
Like this?' A couple of tears slide down my cheeks, the relief of crying
Silently is almost comforting.

I can't look to my past for warmth and solace, most of my memories
Are too painful and embarrassing; and I have no future, except just to
Exist up to death's sighs. I could hang on out of a sense of spite towards
'The State', which is my anonymous benefactor; if I die now I'll save
Its begrudging purse thousands of pounds in unpaid benefits.
I want to fantasise about a green oasis in the midst of this emotional
Desolation, and people it with women who I've loved but been rejected by;
I've never known love. In the dream I have three lovers, and they come
To me as lovers, all pain and misunderstanding is erased... eventually I fall
Asleep gratefully.

I'm awakened by the traffic's roar, a WPC stands over me speaking into
Her walkie-talkie. I notice that she has nice legs...

Phil Fletcher. 1994.

....

GJWA. (Grape Juice With Alcohol.)

If at first sleep doesn't succeed...then sleep some more...
If you can get off again that is.
And yet, if sleep won't come at all, and you haven't got the
Courage to go out THERE!...then I haven't really got any advice
To offer you, except perhaps to drink some more wine in the dead
Of night...if your stomach can stand it. On certain nights where
I live there's a breeze blowing, or the wind is up, or it's raining,
Blowing it against my windowpanes. And when I go for a piss
At 3am, I can tune into the sounds of the natural night.

Nature is attempting to clean up after one more soulless, dirty,
Human day, but the culprits will be up and about long before Nature
Can hope to have any real effect; she's under contract to a

Multi national company called 'NEGLECT'. They're giving her
More work to do for less pay, they don't give a shit, they think she can
Be replaced.
But she makes the sweetest sounds at 3am, there's nothing to compare
With them, unless I hit upon a really good dream where disbelief is
Totally suspended and participation is all that counts. Those dreams
Are so precious, and so rarely remembered or even glimpsed.
I could live permanently at 3 am; there are so few people about then,
And in summer I could lie beneath the stars and forget about this world of cars and the lunatics that drive them.

Phil Fletcher. 24/12/90. Another one of my infamous Christmases spent in solitary confinement.

...

SEEMINGLY NOTHING...BLOKE ON THE DOLE, AGED 47.75 YEARS.

Another night's soulless sleep, and one more barren day to come.
I live in a social vacuum; they imply I don't fit in by giving me
A wide berth.
I sit on my favourite park bench in the early morning light, watching my dog
Relieving himself in the grass; I must invest in a 'POOPER-SCOOPER'
Some day; but a vicious streak in me hopes that someone who wouldn't
Give me the time of day will skid along on it, thus affording
Themselves a smelly shock.
While he rolls in the dew I work out scenarios for a happy, healthy
Existence; but my plans always involve the co-operation of other people,
Usually women, so they always come to nothing.
An overweight middle-aged woman comes shuffling towards me,
Led by a squat Scottie dog, my dog begins to look alert. She plonks herself
Down at the other end of my bench, muttering to herself.
My dog sniffs her dog's behind, her dog tries to bite his nose off,
A yapping and snarling contest ensues; I can't be bothered to call mine off,
And she seems to be preoccupied. The two canines get tired of each other
And go off in different directions. The hopeless case stares straight ahead,
Telling somebody off who only she can see.
Even the birds are in a bad mood, scrapping in the trees.
The early morning sunshine is overtaken by clouds and a few
Spots of rain; I might as well go home and back to bed
For a couple of hours. (The unshaven) Phil Fletcher. 1994.

And now to end this final collection on a disturbing note, a very short piece entitled: 'WIDEAWAKE NIGHTMARE'.

When I'm feeling down, (which is all too often), I see glimpses of a hellish eternity; I hope it's not meant for me? It's either a limitless, desolate and empty black and grey terrain, or, vast and echoey mausoleums, with an indefinable sense of dread at the entrance of each new cavernous, black corridor.

Phil Fletcher. 25/2/06. This is the very end of the very end. 10/4/06.

……………………………………………………………………………..

(Very last update, 17/7/06. If you're reading this, Hi! If you've got any comments I hope the only way you can contact me will be by e-mail. If I've offended anybody's sensitivities I don't want their red angry faces stuck in front of me; I also want to create an air of mystery about myself. See ya.)

………………………………………………………………………………..

This addition is so 'hot' I can't put it on my blog, I probably shouldn't even be using the library computer to type it up on; they've got a blocking policy on 'dodgy' web sites. I categorise my material as 'adult', you'll come acroos equally raw material on TV, on programmes like 'SWINGING' on Channel 5, and The Charlotte Church Show (didn't she used to be 'the voice of an angel'?) on Channel 4:

UPWARDLY MOBILE. Or UPWARDLY THRUSTING. 10-11/10/06.

If I was a good-looking, well hung young man today, and with my attitude As it is now, I'd think everything was going my way after spotting a recent Advert in 'METRO' where people are offering a lot of money for 'me' to have 'My' way with willing young women…on film.

And when I wasn't doing that I could be doing escort work (ads from the Same source), getting paid for having sex with mature business women who Know what they want; saying to them beforehand, 'I don't want scratch Marks down my back or across my arse cheeks, I don't want to get an Infection from whatever's under your finger nails. Your best bet's to let me Ram it into you from behind after I've helped you unwind with the end Of a vibrator up your number two flue; you'll be ripping the pillow to Shreds with your teeth before I've finished with you.'

If we dispense with the flimsy belief that women are the gentler and weaker Sex, now that by and large, the hex of unwanted pregnancies has been Removed from them by the 'morning after pill'; we're seeing more and More examples of them filling their kinky boots with lustful gratification; Girl sex power rules the nation.

A couple of years ago there was a week-long series of programmes on Channel 4 (where else?) on female psychology; the only image that Remains in my mind from this series is of a certain young lady relating About a sex session she had where she was on top and had a massive Orgasm with her man, only to discover once she'd come back down to Earth, a big turd in the bed. She didn't exactly say it was hers, but it Was implied.

If that had been me, I'd have been horrified and mortified at the Same time, to have gone from the transports of delight to seeing A big pile of shite curled up on my silk or satin sheet, which I would Have had to throw out…along with the offender; no matter how Intense a person's ecstasy might be, you can't tell me they could Confuse it with the same sensations as having a crap! Especially When they're on someone's lap!

The 'swinging 60s' has got nothing on today, and none of it's Coming my way; okay so I'm old and grey by UK standards, Without the advantage of Cary Grant-type good looks, I've Still got a few good fucks left in me; the problem is having No one to have them with. From this disabled person's Point of view, life's a pile of poo when it comes to getting my End away; I've had to go 6000 miles away to do this. The only problem now is that when I'm there, I look for Romance amid the glare of the lurid nightlife. A 'wife' And a quiet life would suit me fine…in the hot sunshine.

………………………………………………………………………………

There, I think I've got away with it, and like I wrote in my diary the other day, I'd rather gag and muzzle my brain than create anything else, unless I was getting paid for it; and the chances of that are as remote as ever; maybe when I move to Thailand I'll have better luck?

Phil 'the hot rod' Fletcher. 14/10/06.

www.ingramcontent.com/pod-product-compliance
Lightning Source LLC
Chambersburg PA
CBHW051710040426
42446CB00008B/813
* 9 7 8 0 9 5 5 6 8 7 9 2 1 *